I0410441

THERE ARE OTHER BLACK
SONS TO SAVE

MAKING BLACK LIVES MATTER
BY OVERCOMING THE N-WORD

Let's Stop the Making of Bad-Actors by Bad-Actors in Charge!

Jan Lightfoot, PhD

There Are Other Black Sons to Save
Jan Lightfoot, PhD
©2016, 2017 By Jan Lightfoot, PhD
All rights reserved.

ISBN-13: 978-1539347781
ISBN-10: 1539347788
Also available in eBook

Cover Image © Copyright: www.123rf.com/profile_innovatedcaptures
Prepared for publication by The Author's Mentor
www.TheAuthorsMentor.com

Vinedwellers Ministries, Inc.
Houston, TX

www.janlightfootphd.yolasite.com

Contact Dr. Lightfoot at:
DrJanLightfoot@gmail.com

PUBLISHED IN THE UNITED STATES OF AMERICA

Dedications

To my beloved sons: Brandon and Justin Christopher: You gave me the motivation to get up out of my bed of sickness and despair to live again. I am proud of you and love you more than life.

To Rev. Doctor James E. Lightfoot: Dear Departed Dad, I'd cringe when you'd say, "I hate dumb Ronies, especially my kind." That sounded so harsh then, but now I understand what you meant. I too was Roni but you gave me a chance to change my life when you adopted me. I changed and so can Roni! I pray this book will stop the senseless killing of my people and help to awaken us to God. At least I've tried. I will always love you, Dad!

To Dr. Victor Hirsch: You helped me to look inside myself to integrate at a deeper level and to release my agony through writing this book. Thank you Dr. Hirsch!

To Dr. Elizabeth Gailbraith: Thank you friend for listening to my ranting until I got this out and thanks for helping me to shape these agonizing ideas into an awareness that may help someone.

To Reverend Jerome Stinson: Thank you for the courage and support you gave to me in completing this book in writing and within myself.

To Dr. & Mrs. B. Wesley Austin, Jr.: You supported me as a woman in ministry when no one else would and gave me guidance throughout my pastoral ministry. Thank you Pastor & Mrs. Myra!

To Dr. Paige Patterson, President, Southwestern Theological Seminary: You admonished me to awaken my own people to God, since failure to do so would be slothfulness as a hunter who takes his prey and does not roast it because he leaves it in the field to rot (Proverbs 12: 26-28, May 2015). I won't leave my learning to rot in the field, but I will teach truth that makes us free, especially to my own people. Thank you Dr. Patterson!

To my CPE Class and Memorial Herman Medical Center, especially Carlos Sanchez, Arashal Ryals, Mike Patterson, Rick Chandler, and Keith Rodgers for helping me to claim my own pastoral identity and to identify my ministry purpose.

Special Dedication

To Big Mama: Missionary Lillie Belle Lightfoot (1916-1973): When I asked you, "What's a Roni?" you said, "Anyone who does not love or respect God, themselves or others." You taught me that Roni is not about a color, but about a character and anyone can be one. You said, "Always remember you are just as good as everybody else," because you knew the world would try to teach me that I am inferior. You said, "Don't worry about what everybody else is doing; you do right and God will bless you!" You taught me to do what is right so that I would not live beneath the privileges that God gives by opening doors that no one can shut!" Since I didn't learn that Roni was about color or about me as a person of color, I am not negatively affected by the color definition of Roni, although I am affected by the mistreatment of all black people by inclusion of all of us as Ronies. You taught me who I am and taught me how to demonstrate who I am; so I learned that good character transcends color because you taught me to do what is right, lovely, and true. Now I am carrying this message to others to do what's right to see God bless and vindicate us. It worked for me! So I believe it will work for others! Thank You—My Beloved Big Mama! I will always love you.

Special Acknowledgements

To The Board Members of Vine Dweller's Ministries, Inc.: Bishop C. Edward Moten, CEO/Covering; Minister Darryl Staggers, Mediator; Elder Linda Dearman, Christian Education & Training; Rev. Jerome Stinson, Security Officer; Minister Linda Brown and Rev. Kenneth Jackson, Prayer Ministry: Thank you for your prayers, care, and advisement in the vision and mission of this ministry.

To Bishop K. B. Spears: When I gave up on living in a Mental Hospital, you came and got me out and reunited my fingers with the Hammond organ and I found provision and purpose for living. Thank you for being a pastor who cares!

To Ida Delaney and to all of the named and unnamed, armed and unarmed Black men, women, and boys and girls who have been injured or killed by white men and by bully lawmen due to wrongful collateral damage and racist terrorism against Black people in America.

To one woman, Toya Graham[1], who rightly stood against bad-acting with her son as we know to do, but have seemingly forgotten? Good job, Mom!

To My Own People: We are a resilient people who have lost our way. I pray that this book will help to bring us back to where we belong and bring about a change that will cause us to treat ourselves, other people, and God as we should. Thereby we will reciprocate this same treatment rather than making ourselves targets against terror and antagonism. We cannot simply say that our lives matter, but we must know and show that our lives matter and when our lives matter to ourselves, by demonstration, then our lives will matter to society as well.

Black Lives Matter,
"Actions speak louder than words!"

---

[1] CBS News. Baltimore mom: "I just lost it" seeing son at riots with rock in hand. (2015, April 29). Retrieved September 11, 2016, from http://www.cbsnews.com/news/baltimore-mom-toya-graham-on-smacking-son-at-riots-freddie-gray/

*Let's stop the making of bad-actors
by bad-actors in charge!*

THERE ARE OTHER BLACK

SONS TO SAVE

MAKING BLACK LIVES MATTER
BY OVERCOMING THE N-WORD

TABLE OF CONTENTS

Writing Style

The run-on and poor grammar style of this work is not to promote "Ebonics," but is intentional in order to soften the blow of the content perhaps making it more readable, less shocking, and helpful. Also, this was a rush job; so please excuse any grammatical errors. I hope it's clear enough for you to get the point. So pardon me, but I've got other work to get to. Thanks!

Disclaimer: Generalizations made in this book are not intended to describe the whole, but are stated as all because of the preponderance of occurrences that causes a particular group, practice, or category to represent the whole through creation of the deception that the some or most equals the whole.

WHO IS JAN LIGHTFOOT AND
WHY IS SHE WRITING THIS BOOK?

I am a Black woman who is also the mother of two precious black sons. I struggled with what Dad meant when expressing his disgust with certain people until two experiences opened my eyes. First, I was racially profiled by a security officer at a Chick-Fil-A who saw me as an NWord and treated me that way. Secondly, I suffered the abuse of power by a so-called pastor, theologically trained at an accredited seminary, who failed to teach parishioners what he'd learned, instead taught parishioners to think and act like NWords. So, I understand how we are fashioned to become NWords by our leaders and how this fashioning leads to racism against us. Racism is terrorism against us but I believe we can minimize racist terrorism when we are in right standing with God.

I am writing this book from a black perspective, but moreover, I am writing as a Black mother with two Black sons. I come recommending Six Lessons to remedy us from being formed and targeted as NWords, as I taught my black sons. I taught my sons how to avoid the injustice of the law by obeying the law. Consequently, they know how to minimize the negative effects of being young, gifted, and Black. When I see the killings and beatings of young Black men, I am mortified and grieved. Although my sons know how to deescalate trouble, they too can become victims of wrongful collateral damage by law enforcement. Sadly, all black people are targets of this evil. Yet, we must teach our sons how to avoid becoming targets of racists as my Big Mama taught me. We can minimize the effect of being perceived as NWords.

Thus, I am writing this book to teach other sons (and daughters) because it seems no one is teaching us. I never allowed my sons to focus on what other people were doing, but to focus on what *they, themselves* were doing, because we cannot control anyone other than ourselves. I want other sons (and daughters) to know how to save themselves from trouble and how to be successful in the world. I hope this book helps to end the senseless brutality against and killing of Black people. Lastly, I am my brother's (sister's) keeper and ALL lives matter, even Roni's life. Therefore, I am writing this book to teach other sons (and daughters) what I learned. I saved my precious sons from racist injustice but there are other black sons to save.

PROLOGUE : SETTLING THE N-WORD MATTER

That "some folks are N......," is a bitter true fact,
    But WE all know a N...... isn't necessarily a Black.
They come in yellow, red, brown, and white, too.
    N...... isn't about a look, but about the things folks do.
Calling somebody a N...... is about their conduct,
    Only KKK thinkers are talking about a construct.
Nobody sane names folks by the way they look.
    N...... is about people not following The Good Book.
N...... don't respect other folks or themselves,
    They have no sense of obligation to do things well,
They ignore good manners and common courtesy,
    They disregard all attempts to avert controversy.
The only thing they understand is death and fear,
    And some don't get it until a piece of steel is near,
Not grasping respect, they only respond to threats,
    And concrete profane language that is brain direct.
They'll give you no problems once they know,
    You'll kick their butts and show them the door.
Since a word is a conceptualization of an observation,
    That doesn't just come out of nowhere from bliss,
Like so, the N-Word wouldn't ever have developed,
    Had an identifying behavior never demonstrated it,
So you can't stop anybody from saying a word,
    When its existence in reality is clear and well known!
And you can't tell society to stop saying "N......,"
    When the manifestation of the word is being shown!
Fact is some people are N...... and anybody can be,
    But a N...... doesn't have to be either you or me!

PURPOSE

Righteousness exalts a nation, but sin is a disgrace to any people, (even to the best of people). The King's favor is toward a servant who acts wisely, but his anger is toward him who acts shamefully (Proverbs 14: 34 and 35: NASB).

Although all racial groups have a share of bad-acting individuals, I am concerned that disproportionate numbers of my racial group are disenfranchised from the American pursuit of life, liberty and happiness, and I hope to awaken my own people to God. This can only be achieved through depending on God as our forefathers did, not resorting to lawlessness. Thus this book was written to:

- Teach my people what I learned from my grandmother and thereby transmitted to my sons to raise us up;
- Stop Wrongful (targeting the whole and getting some) and Normal Collateral Damage (targeting a few and getting some) upon my people;
- Expose and Stop the Order of the Day to kill all of us;
- Stop the Making of Bad-Actors by Bad-Actors In-Charge;
- Stop Us from Causing Us to be Targets of Terror;
- Stop Us from Hurting Us;
- Stop American Racist Terrorism against Blacks in America;
- Promote Love and Righteous Living;

- To Promote that, "Black Lives Matter," but no value can matter outside its representation that negates it. Therefore, if we want to matter individually we must look better collectively and show more character than we show color since *Action Speaks Louder Than Words*. Until then, "What do we do about Roni's terror upon America?"
- To focus on what "we" are doing rather than what "they" are doing;
- Deconstruct the misrepresentation of Black people by NWords –(bad-actors of similar physical characteristics);
- Deconstruct the misrepresentation of love by false pretense;
- Deconstruct the misrepresentation of God by Christians;
- To eliminate the generalization of hatred against Blacks;
- To awaken my own people to God.

CHAPTER 1   WHAT IS RONI?

RONI IS A WORD SUBSTITUTION

Roni has been affectionately substituted for the N-Word by the author—who fondly renamed "Roni." She loves Roni and says she was a Roni, too, but she has learned how to act so that her actions will not bring harm to herself from people or predicaments. When speaking of Roni in a less favorable perspective she refers to Roni as "Certain People." She wants other Ronies (who come in all colors and are in all places) to learn how to act so they can be successful and happy like her through learning at least Six Lessons. She believes, "If I did it, anybody can." She wasn't born with a silver spoon in her mouth and is not some bougie-Roni who doesn't know about the School of Hard Knocks, manipulation, misuse, or racism. So, she wants to let us know that we have the power to change how we demonstrate ourselves to the world. She knows all of us are Roni's, but some of us don't know when and where to act out of character with whom we really are—Children of the King. She says she is in recovery from being formed into Roni and on occasion can act like Roni, but only by her own will. She knows how to walk among Ronies without becoming a part of Roni, but is begging for some help to destroy the false belief that all black people behave as Ronies. This must first start with some "act-right" within the culture group. Firstly, this book is dedicated to this purpose—help Roni to understand the value of living right.

Roni is a pet name. I have lovingly substituted "Roni" for the N-Word; also the prototype of "a wrongdoer." I use this euphemism as an indirect or mild expression presented as a replacement for the N-Word in consideration of the harshness and offensiveness of this word. Roni is a nickname to soften the blow of the N-Word in order to offer lessons in overcoming the N-Word. I use *Roni, NWord, Certain People, bad-actors,* and *N...* interchangeably throughout the text as a replacement out of love and respect to my Ronies. I dare not fall into indifference or being unloving.

RONI AS COLLATERAL DAMAGE

This book is being written to awaken society to the dreadful assault against persons of Negroid descent in America due to a lop-sided appearance of all deception that causes Black people to wrongly suffer for what Roni does. As a Black author, I purpose to help my people to look at what we can do to love and respect ourselves so that we will not present ourselves as a threat to society that has resulted in an Order of the Day—America's collective conscience sanctioning the killing of all Black people while targeting our bad-actors who appear to be the predominate number of our race. We are the only ones who can put a stop to the making of bad-actors by bad-actors in charge. This contributes to Wrongful Collateral Damage and American Terrorism against Black People, leading us into the destruction of our own. We are self-destructing while sustaining a self-perpetuating subculture of ignorance, bad-acting, and poverty.

I know "the system" bears the greater blame, but if we do our part, the negative effects of "the system" will be decreased drastically and we will be less likely to be injured by those who hate and are fearful of us. Also, the law will be more accountable to protect us. Right now, I'm just trying to get *us* to stop hurting *us*—we should not add to what society is allowing and doing to intentionally hurt us—Wrongful Collateral Damage. Wrongful Collateral Damage (opposed to "normal" Collateral Damage) is occurrences of injuries and killings of Blacks that are not incidental; rather they are planned and intentional. Normal or customary Collateral Damage is incidental and conjunctions that occur alongside the main intention. Both types of collateral damage seem intentional because "the system" is not trying to control Black people; it is trying to control N-Words but is inadvertently killing Black people in the process of trying to nullify Roni-terrorism of America. And we do appear as a terror, sad to say. All in all, social order must be maintained.

American society may be somewhat blinded into thinking that recent incidents in the media have been unintentional or unplanned. Therefore, we are not focused on the reason this (normal) Collateral Damage occurs in the first place—[incidental injuries and deaths that happen to an unintended target in the course of controlling or stopping an intended target]. Both types are purposed to control crime and bad-actors but we see this as a Black problem when it is a Roni problem.

DOES RONI'S LIFE MATTER?

This misconception is demonstrated with the saying, "Black Lives Matter." However, this slogan doesn't isolate the problem of Wrongful Collateral Damage because wrongful or abnormal collateral damage is intentional to target the whole to get at a few, whereas normal or customary Collateral Damage is incidental to targeting the few. Unfortunately, the slogan, "Black Lives Matters," lumps all person of color into a group for which the target population is aimed, but fact is, Roni's lives should matter, as well. The problem is that all Black people are seen as Roni but in reality neither Black lives, nor Roni's lives, matter when Wrongful Collateral Damage is applied—all become the target. We all know that all lives matter but the problem we face is how to control Roni. Do we just kill all black people to control and rid ourselves of Roni? Does Roni's life matter?

Order of the Day?

Understanding the Order of the Day: To Exterminate without Discrimination (or without making a distinction between the good and the bad).

"If we kill *all* of them (that look alike), then we'll be sure to kill the bad ones too!"

In response to the wrongful killings of Black people through law enforcement brutality and hate crimes the campaign has been launched that, "Black Lives Matter." This slogan doesn't capture the reality that is creating the wrongful deaths against Black people who have become targets as a whole. Everyone already knows that Black lives matter—actually all lives matter—but again, the underlying question in unawareness and in society's collective conscience[2] is "What can society do to control bad-actors (Ronies) who look like Black citizens?" Since society doesn't know the difference between N-Words and Black citizens, in the course of targeting *N-Word-bad-actors*, society is incidentally injuring and killing all Black citizens, as well as N-Words, because the Order of the Day is to *kill all of us who present any possible or imagined threat. A*nd this is based on the way we look—our color not our character. The blindness of thinking, "Everything black is a N......," is causing us to be profiled, stereotyped, and discriminated when we have done nothing wrong. I will talk about an experienced I had of this nature in the furtherance of this book. Briefly, I experienced racial injustice at a Chick-Fil-A, which calls itself a Christian

---

[2] The set of shared beliefs, ideas and moral attitudes which operate as a unifying force within society. The term was introduced by the French sociologist Émile Durkheim in 1893 (*Collins Dictionary of Sociology*, p93).

organization. Yet, a bully sheriff on duty as a security guard was allowed by the manager to badger, bully, and insult me about my handicap placard because he saw me as a N-word trying to get one over by illegally parking. He was wrong but could have injured or killed me because of his racist attitude against me.

BLACK VS. RONI?

We can minimize the confusion between *Black citizens* and *Black-citizen-look-alikes* who are bad-actors, or N-Words (herewith named Roni), if we'd clarify two facts in the minds of the populace which are: (1) that Roni and Black are not the same; (2) that some or most doesn't mean all; and (3) that we understand the Order of the Day and know how to stop society from killing us through the righteous living. This will deconstruct the misrepresentation of Black people by NWords.

This book aims to stop the Order of the Day, which is, to *exterminate all Black people without discrimination in response to Roni's terrorism of America and American "racist terrorism" against all People of Negroid blood (which includes Roni).* Right now, the target is upon appearance that includes N-Words and Black law-abiding citizens; so all Black people are a target— even the President of the United States in 2016. It is obvious that society doesn't know President Obama is not an N-Word and is thereby treating him in like manner, although he has been an exemplary man and a good president whereas Donald Trump depicting behavior of an NWord is not viewed this way being wealthy and white, though he demonstrates NWords do come in all colors.

Kill all of us, even when we are in a church?
The Order of the Day to *kill all of us* is dominating the thoughts of Americans as demonstrated in Charleston, South Carolina; the shooter learned this hatred from someone. Question is, "Who?" His parents? Media? Hate Groups? His Peers? His Mind? Satan?

Roni: Generalized to ALL of us?

This Order of the Day lumps all persons of Negroid descent/blood as N-Words. In other words, society (including Black America,) is trying to target N-Words, but are incidentally hurting and killing Black citizens in the process. Citizens are not the intended targets but may be the sad cost of controlling crime and maintaining order—collateral damage—that is out of hand. This is due to blindness in society whereby *Black* has been made one and the same with N-Words.

All of us need to halt the activities of N-Words for the sake of all, this include Black citizens,[3] who also and primarily suffer the activities of N-Words. So, we know that Black lives matter, but so do the lives of N-Words, but the question is, *"What do we do about these bad-actors so that all Black people are not categorized as Ronies?"* Do we just let grown White people like Zimmerman kill anyone—even children—and justify it saying *the child appeared to be potentially dangerous to society* or do we allow the police to exterminate without discrimination (like the military term "terminate with extreme prejudice"[4]) which means *kill all*?

Why Six Lessons for Roni?

Targeting *all* black people is the wrong way to manage the disproportionate numbers of bad-actors among Black Americans, namely, N-Words. I believe we can ameliorate the vast problem now of Wrongful Collateral Damage against Black citizens if we clarify that the target are N-Words not all Black people and then teach these folks how to act. I am proposing Six Lessons that we

---

[3] Citizen defined: a person who legally belongs to a country and has the rights and protection of that country; Retrieved on May 8, 2015 from: [http://www.merriam-webster.com/dictionary/citizen].

[4] In military intelligence, an order to assassinate or to execute. Its meaning was explained in a *New York Times* report on an incident during the Vietnam War. Also quoted by Smith, Terence (August 14, 1969). "Details of Green Beret Case Are Reported in Saigon."

must teach to our sons and daughters to save them from becoming unable to compete in the world and to save them from becoming targets for bullets, jails, prison and lying on their backs to make a living (flat-backing). We must insist upon these lessons to be followed in all social systems: schools, work, leisure, sports, law enforcement, and prison/jail systems. Don't look for anyone else to teach the youth; you teach them when you get them under your authority and make them follow these lessons or put them out! Learning these Six Lessons will obstruct the wrongful killings of Blacks in America. We can't make any progress unless we master these Six Lessons—discussed throughout this book. I'm going to reveal these simple lessons very soon. They are the missing link to our civility and Christianity. Don't get it twisted!

> THESE SIX LESSONS ARE THE MISSING LINK TO OUR CIVILITY AND CHRISTIANITY.
> DON'T GET IT TWISTED!

BUT FIRST - BLACK DOES NOT EQUAL NIGGER

I know America is blind as to *who* Black citizens are, because I experienced this with a so-called *lawman* who would not see or hear what I was saying because he viewed me as an N-Word due to the color of my skin. I will explain this in more detail further in this book. This target or *identification blindness* (inability to discern difference between a citizen and a criminal due to racial prejudice rather than the demonstration of character) is dangerous to us. In other words, I was the N-Word to this man because I am Black. This caused him to treat me like I was an N-Word and place me in danger of Wrongful Collateral Damage and Terrorism. In the collective consciousness of White American superiority all black persons are inferior to whites but the American collective consciousness needs to understand…

"Everything Black is NOT a NIGGER!"

After we are able to differentiate between color and character then we can address what to do about N-Words, but lumping everybody who looks alike together is unacceptable. So, trust me, I know firsthand what's going on with "the system" and I am working on some things that "the system" does against us because I know how it wrongly effects innocent citizens and mistreats those who are *guilty* or *innocent* with cruel and unusual punishment. I know it keeps us down and I know that it polices those it criminalizes, but this book addresses what we, as the Black race, are doing to bring harm upon ourselves and make things worse for us. Have you read my book, *Caesar Took My Cheese*? I know about these wicked systems—family, school, work, the church, law-enforcement and certainly the government—but we are not excused for what we do because of what anybody else does. As we know, *"Two wrongs don't make a right."* We are responsible for what we do and must take responsibility for our actions.

HOW RONI MISREPRESENTS BLACKS

Come on now, we may look like the worst acting of all the bad-actors, because we are good at everything we do, even when it comes to bad-acting. And our kids are the worst of the bad-actors in the schools. We are our own worst enemy and I want to stop this partly self-inflicted pain of racist terrorism against us because of what we do. We don't need to worry about what anyone else is doing to our cultural group, as much as we need to worry about what we are doing against ourselves. We need to do what is right in the eyes of God and see God bless us. That is what I did. I did what was right and listened to God and God blessed me and at times, I was terrible. I was out of the race

14

before the race got started and I was behind the starting line before I got started. Yet, God pulled me out of the pits of despair, out of turmoil and disdain and put me on the mountaintop. And you can follow the same path to success by doing what is right by God, yourself and others and walking and talking with God and obeying Him.

Previously in my life I was an *overt threat*, living unprotected. I was exposed because I was not doing right by myself, God, and others. With God's help I became a *covert threat* by doing right by myself, others, and God. An individual or group is a covert threat when the individual or group does right by themselves, others, and God and is empowered to be adept in all areas of life whereby one's spirit is untouchable, protected, and defended against racism, abuse, and hatred. I received God's protection by obeying Him.

WHAT KIND OF THREAT ARE YOU?

Right now, Black people are an *overt threat* to society and that's why society allows White folks and the police to kill us, hurt us and mistreat us. *If we* were to become a covert threat we'd put a stop to this Wrongful Collateral Damage used to hold Roni at bay. We know we've got to hold Roni down or else there'll be a *Roni-takeover* that will ruin the earth. If we would do what is *right* then God would be on our side, but right now we have no regard for God and we are on the losing side—The Dark Side.

But we can turn this around and be blessed if we will just: (1) admit wrong doings; (2) believe in ourselves and know that each and every one of us are a work in progress working toward becoming our best; and (3) do what is right by ourselves, others, and God and God *will* help us. I know this because I considered myself a Roni, but God changed my name. [*Do not let this Book of the Law depart from your mouth; meditate on it day and night, so that you may be careful to do everything written in it. Then you will be prosperous and successful. (Josh 1:8; NIV)*]. I didn't believe bad things people tried to make me believe about myself and I did what's right by me, others, and God and God blessed me. He will do the same for you!

Are You in the Roni-making Business?

I cannot participate in making other Ronies feel helpless or allow us to cast blame because I was never allowed to be made to feel helpless or hopeless. I was not a victim of *learned helplessness*[5] because I learned that I *cannot* choose my family, but I *can* choose my friends and I learned that although me being taken advantage of, neglected, or abused was not my fault it was my problem and only I could get help to fix the problems I was left with. When I started seeking the truth and seeking help, I met a traveler every now and then, who showed me *the light* and I followed it.

So, if I turn my back on Roni, I'll be turning my back on myself. And "Oh yes," I can very well step away from Roniland because I've got knowledge and experience under my belt to change my environment. I'm in Roniland (co-existing with a group of Ronies) now, but I can move around. First, I must try to help Roni to get skinny and hopefully to not exist. Wishful thinking, I know, but I still want to try. I cannot participate with Roni-making and since silence gives consent, I must speak out and hope that someone will listen. Anyway, I'll just do my part and leave the results up to God.

I don't want to make Ronies and neither do I want to participate in Roni-making or in killing Roni when I can teach

---

[5] Learned helplessness occurs when an animal is repeatedly subjected to an aversive stimulus that it cannot escape. Eventually, the animal will stop trying to avoid the stimulus and behave as if it is utterly helpless to change the situation. Even when opportunities to escape are presented, this learned helplessness will prevent any action (From: http://psychology.about.com/od/lindex/f/earned-helplessness.htm; May 7, 2015).

Roni to not put him or herself in the position of absorbing the fall-out of terror caused by bad actors, whether real, or imagined. I am focused and ready to teach and consult in the hardcore fashion needed. However, I know that I can only teach the Black Ronies who are ready to change! I love Roni because I was *Roni*, too. So, I can teach Roni how to not absorb the wrong teaching by Ronies-In-Charge that keep Roni in Roniland and unequipped for a world that requires excellence and discipline. If Ronies want to present themselves as a Roni, then I want this is to occur by choice and not by chance. Each individual must decide if they want to be a Roni, because the nature of Roni is inherent within our basic human carnal nature. And all of us can be a Roni if we choose to say and do what is natural. But our God-given mandate is to transform from what is natural to become who and what we are *supernaturally*.

WILL YOU BE THE POOR RONI?

It works the same way in being poor. Yes, someone in America is going to be poor, but each one must decide if it will be you. If Roni wants to be poor then I want Roni to make an informed decision to be poor, not to be tricked, manipulated, and deceived by the Ronies-In-Charge into becoming Ronies-In-Unawareness. That's not right! So, I want to help Roni to work Roni out of Roni so that Roni can become like the King and not like the Ronies who are reproducing, benefiting from, and destroying Roni.

Moreover, when it comes to teaching Roni, you cannot simply *teach* or *tell*, you must *show* by enforcing the rules because Roni has been able to slip and slide so long until he doesn't know that his mind isn't even entertaining teaching. So, when you teach Roni, you must have the power to reject him and put him out, because that's the only thing Roni understands. Society talks about *Leaving-No-Child-Behind* and the only way to teach Roni is to leave his butt behind, IF he will not follow the rules so he'll get it, want to be a part of it, or get put out so that he won't hold the others back who don't want to be left behind.

We've got to go back to the basis and teach the Six Lessons or else nobody is going to learn anything no matter how good the teacher or teaching. Those who are in-charge must require students, subordinates, parishioners, parents, and inmates to follow the recommended Six Lessons (forthcoming). You can't just do whatever you want to do whenever you want to do it, however you want to; not if you want to be successful.

You've got to tell Ronies...

To stay in this house (this home, school, church, choir, or job) everybody's got to act right!
I said, "To stay up in here everybody's got to act right,
Whether you ARE right is between you and God,
But whether you ACT right is between you and I,
I don't care if you are blind, crippled or crazy,
to stay here you've got to act right, Precious Heart!
If not, you can go to,
The church house,
The jail house,
The outhouse,
The nut house,
Or you don't have to go to yo house,
But you've got to get up out of here,
If you can't act right go whisper in God's ear,
You've got to have Acceptable Conduct To Stay—(ACTS),
So, if you can't act right please go about your way,
Or close your mouth and go sit down somewhere and pray,
Cause everybody's got to act right up in here, to stay!

How can you to take a child or anyone somewhere they don't want to go? People talk about *no child left behind*, when they need to say, "If you don't *act right* your behind will be left behind and out of this school (home, job, club, church, choir, training, sports team)." *This is why the Good Book says to resist the devil and he will flee and Roni ain't nothing but the devil, everywhere he goes.* So, doing right is *the key* to overcoming Roni and since I am accountable only for what I do in the Kingdom, I must do what I was destined to do—to put myself on blast or even to shame so that I may rescue some and hopefully rescue many. After all, I was already

> REMEMBER WHEN READING THIS, THAT RONI STANDS FOR THE N-WORD (N.......).

groomed for this by living a life of shame among Ronies for something I didn't do and had no knowledge of what I was supposed to have done. Consequently, I've been walking over fifty years alone with the King and I can walk the rest of the way alone, rather than to walk with a fool.

UNDERSTANDING RONI TALK

Although, I am well able to handle the English language with clarity, for the sake of softening the content of what I am about to say, I've intentionally used and will explain the foregoing using poor grammar, run-on sentences, incomplete sentences, and made-up words. A glossary is included in the back of the book to explain these definitions and to clarify invented words contained therein. Remember when reading this that Roni stands for the N-Word.

Roni-making is the making of Ronies by so-called Roni leaders and this process has nothing to do with non-Ronies, but has everything to do with Ronies in charge of the church, Ronies who say they are community leaders, and bad-acting Ronies who have been made into sports and TV stars. In other words, "White folks ain't got nothing to do with it." Roni-making is a *Black thing* although Roni-breaking is a *White thing* or *rich-folks thing*. I hope Ronies will stop making Ronies for White Ronies to use and kill and I hope White Ronies will learn that *some* does not mean *all*! One thing is for sure, "We is all Ronies," whether Yellow, Red, Brown, Black or White, because of sin. Yet, some of us know we can't act like that, because we must act like the King.

After meeting an anti-defamation lawyer while flying back home from a mini-vacation, I was further inspired to write this book for the main purpose of lifting Roni to where Roni belongs. I said to the lawyer, "I'm happy to hear what anti-defamation efforts are doing to raise civil tolerance and equality, but what does intolerance and inequality have to do with bad-acting and crime? Especially Roni-on-Roni crime and Ronies looting, killing, shooting with guns, and rioting against our own kind? I'd like to see an Anti-Immorality League."

If possible, poor Dr. King must be spinning in his grave with disgust to know Ronies are making Ronies and causing hatred against all of us who look like Roni from bigots in charge, and this Roni-making is being done in his name and in Jesus' name! Consequently, this book was written to help Roni in five ways to:

1. Wake-Up: To wake Roni up to know how Roni has been conditioned into not being whom the King created him or her to be and to help Roni turn away from what the church, TV, government, media and the State are doing to shape him or her into Roni. So, telling about who I used to be is to wake us up so we can accept responsibility for who we are, what we represent and fulfill the purpose of why we were put on this earth—to help some, not to hurt.

2. Get-up: To lift Roni through educating not through eradicating Roni, in order to avoid messing up society and making trouble for Roni-lookalikes. So, telling about who I used to be is for the purpose of holding Roni at bay in the right way. I am promoting Six Lessons that must be insisted upon by those of us who are in charge so that we may teach the missing link to our safety and success. We must promote a zero tolerance for failure to demonstrate these principles.

3. Listen-up: To inform Roni on how to *undo* the *doing* of Roni-making. Thereby we will stop our participation in Roni-making. I hope to help Roni to understand that American society has caused us to forget our values because we have become a part of the melting pot that lies to us about what it takes for us to achieve success in America. We have lost our identity and sense of reality. We have accepted the lies that anything goes, that we can say and do whatever we want to do, that our opinion and vote matters. This is Democracy but we—King's Kids—are to live in the Theocracy (God's World). This is purposed to raise Roni and societal consciousness to a level of spiritual and secular responsibility, civil tolerance, morality, and equal access for Roni, because you cannot tear down and build up simultaneously, but you can do it one at a time. Roni did not make him or herself, but is a part of an unrealized process that all of society participates—even you! So, telling about who I used to be is intended to shed light on how we can become all God intended for us to become. I must accept the fact that I need to change to make my life what God has intended, but it all starts with listening up!

4. Step-up: To take on any insult to put a dent in Roni (make Roni small) and skinny, and skinnier, and skinnier until there are no Ronies left. So, telling about who I used to be is to make *The Roni* part of me smaller and smaller until Roni is a zero. This will require some tearing down before we can build back up. This Roni thing is so bad until it's like a condemned building. You can't renovate it; you're got to tear it down and rebuild it. We can step up to our rightful place of resilience and rightness, if we will embrace right-living.

Foremost, I wrote this book to help Roni to:

5. Stay-Up: To put a stop to Wrongful and Customary Collateral Damage[6] through the needless killing of Ronies by law enforcement and prejudiced people. This can happen by teaching Roni to *not* give the unknowledgeable, the fearful and the bullies a reason to justify removing Black Americans from the earth's realm, as Collateral Damage (targeting a few and getting some)—a necessary evil for the price of freedom and protection nor through Wrongful Collateral Damage (targeting the whole to get some). So, last but not least, telling about whom I was, is to keep us from being destroyed by society through us because, one thing is for sure, we are the devil on ourselves. Roni-making is all about *us's-against-us's*, but we can stop this and this book hopes to at least put a dent in Roni if not to put a stop to Roni, by helping Roni act right.

Then, secondly, we can give people a choice in making informed decisions about where they will land in life. We are not helpless like Ronies-In-Charge fashion us become for *usury of the rich and famous* and *rich and famous want-to-be's*. Hope this book helps!

1st Correction Needed: (OUR NAME or CONSTRUCT)

Before we get started the first thing we need to correct is *us* answering to the wrong name—*African Americans*. We are not Africans! Allowing ourselves to be called the wrong name and answering to it is even more illogical. We are

---

[6] The term "collateral damage" is by definition the unintended injuries, damage, or deaths through action (Scribendi editor comments, Feb. 2015).

better off answering to "Negroes," since we are of Negroid blood. Even more accurate, we are Persons/ Americans of African Descent or Persons/Americans of Negroid Blood, or just Black, not African Americans, which is a misnomer and an oxymoron[7] that mars our identity.

An *oxymoron* is a figure of speech designed to describe an abstract idea not a concrete individual. We have let society describe us as an abstraction, a paradox, a self-contradiction, and an absurdity and citizens, politicians, clerics, educators and community leaders are going along with it. So, this is the first image-killer we need to put a stop to. This needs to be done fairly quickly before we can even get to check our actions because you must know who you are and where you are before you can get to where you need to be. I understand that we cannot control what other folks say about us or about what they call us, but my question is: Why are we answering to a name that is NOT our name? And why are we calling ourselves out of our name?

> WHY ARE WE ANSWERING TO A NAME THAT IS NOT OUR NAME?
>
> DO WE KNOW OUR NAME? I DON'T THINK SO! YOUR NAME IDENTIFIES YOU!

I say to children, if someone is calling you out of your name, why are you answering to it unless you think it's your name? If you know your name, don't answer to any other name. I'm not as bothered about people calling folks out of their name as I am about people answering to the wrong

---

[7] **Re: The African American Misnomer (giving the wrong name to a person, place, or thing):** This is the first error we need to correct and should insist on America changing this error. We are already displaced in America and need not be confused about who we are. We are not Africans. We are not African and American, we are only American and at most Americans or Persons of African Descent/Roots but we are NOT African anything, being born and raised in America. We are Americans whose forefathers came from Africa making us of African Descent or Black Americans not African Americans!

name or worst is reacting to a wrong name. We can't control anyone, but ourselves! But we can control what name we answer to if we know who we are. We need to know when people are talking to us and when they are talking to themselves, but the question is: Do we know our name? I don't think so!

2nd Correction Needed: (OUR CONDUCT) After we fix answering to the wrong name then we need to implement Six Lessons and seven more to total 13 Actions that will to decrease America's oppression of and killing of us!

We must correct our CONSTRUCT & CONDUCT. CONSTRUCT by deconstructing our vague identity by correcting (1) what we call ourselves; (2) what we answer to. CONDUCT by avoiding the injustice of the law by obeying it and culturally following the Six Lessons in this book. We must have a zero tolerance against violating these rules and make no excuses. Ronimakers give us excuses and cause us to believe these rules don't matter then they cause our lives to not matter. These Bad-actors in charge make us believe we are excused from acting right as if we can't do for any reason, when the real reason is that we won't do. However, everybody must follow the rules, no matter what because those who CANNOT or WILL NOT will both be isolated and eliminated from the American pursuit of happiness, since law and order and social control is a must for a civilized society! It goes like this:

THE CONDITION	YOUR PROBLEM	THE RESULT You will be:
Can't do	You are crazy	isolated/eliminated/ medicated/ locked up
Won't do	You are criminal	isolated/eliminated incarcerated
Can't lean to do	You are stupid	isolated/ eliminated
Can't do, Won't do, Can't learn to do	You are unable, disabled, not accountable, eligible 4 help/care	isolated/eliminated But OK since you won't know what is happening to you

So, in response to the subject of this chapter, "What is Roni?" Roni can be anyone (any color, creed, or kind) who doesn't love or respect themselves, others, or God but Roni doesn't have to be you or I. Godspeed with this!

CHAPTER 2   THE BLACK-WHITE AMERICAN DIVIDE

Why Write It? *To Expose.*

As a previous Roni, I wrote this book because most of my life experiences have prepared me for opposition. Life has helped me to develop fortitude and I believe I have been divinely prepared to handle the anger and ridicule I expect from writing this book. I wrote it because I truly believe it must be said and believe it will bring about positive results for everyone. Since we are as sick as our secrets, I must expose Roni (Roni, Roni-making, Roni-breaking), from a first person position; only a Black person can say it; so I'm saying it since, *"We are as sick as our secrets!"*

THE BLACK-WHITE AMERICAN DIVIDE

Secrets can be both hidden and open. The hidden secret is that all of us have been branded by society, mainly police as NWords and are wrongly treated accordingly. The open secret is that there is an Black-White American Divide based on appearance, not character, even when character is intact. I saw this divide develop in America with the OJ Simpson case, wherein "they" (whites and those who think they are white) felt as if "we" (blacks in America) were not on the same side of the law and got away with killing one of their own, causing them to be fearful of all of us and thereby not give a care justifying them in taking revenge on all of us because of their connotation that

Black-OJ got away with killing their White-Nicole. White America has been riled-up about this in open secrecy for years 1995 (OJ's acquittal of murder) – 2008 (OJ's conviction of theft). Still the divide has not been healed but has worsened; worsening to the point that they have taken revenge on all black people for what OJ did or didn't do demonstrating that they don't give a da..n about us. This indifferent attitude in America led to society allowing haters, bad guys, and bully cops to kill us as if we are nothing or don't matter. But now our children have taken on the same indifferent attitude saying, "They are going to kill us anyway; so we'll just kill them because we don't give a da..n either." Now we have a Dallas incident wherein five policemen are killed supposedly by a black gunman (2016), if it was this individual because he was killed. But for now we'll take this obvious conclusion that demonstrates, those you terrorize will eventually terrorize you.

Both sides are wrong.

Only God can exercise vengeance justifiably. When we carry out revenge we do so wrongly and create the kind of problem we have in America—the Black-White American Divide. This is a deception because people are not divided by appearance but by socioeconomics and when we fail to factor in this truth, we start stereotyping, discriminating against, racially profiling, racially terrorizing and killing both innocent and guilty persons of the group we are terrorized of. Terror is working against both sides and causing a deadly reaction on both sides. I did not see this divide even with the assignation of Dr. Martin Luther King, because the whole country, save the KKK, was in mourning regarding his death. I saw the divide begin with OJ. This open secret of this Good-Evil situation being misconstrued as a Black-White issue has alienated us via appearance. OJ's situation had nothing to do with race, although society gave it a racial connotation—giving Black the face of evil. This began the construction of all Blacks as NWords and made all us threats and targets of revenge and injustice. And sadly, most people will become as they are treated. I didn't become "whom" I was treated to become, but this is rare. Consequently, I educate people about how to overcome our environment, heredity, and conditioning, because we are God's creations not the creations of our parents, our community, or society. We can remain who we are and not allow the environment to cause us to come out of this character. Terror can change us and cause us to behave in ways inconsistent with whom we are. So, America must stop the terror and all persons, on both sides of the color line must demonstrate the lessons recommended in this book to bring us back to where we belong.

TERROR DISPENSED UPON BLACKS

1995: OJ Acquittal *(Evil-Good Issues become Black-White Issue)*

1995: Present Black becomes Evil and targets of revenge

1996: Passing Gun Laws *(Aimed to kill thieves, thugs mostly Black and Mexican NWords)*

2009: Present Open Disrespect for 1st Black President

2012: America Sanctions the Killing of Black Sons by Legal System/ Bully Cops/Racist *(Ex: Trevon Martin Killing)*

2012: Legal Wrongdoing *(Everything Black is a Nigger Attitude = The Law wasn't made to help Blacks attitude from cops)*

2012 - 2015: Killing of Black Sons and Daughters by Bully cops

2015 - 2016: The Law is Unreliable

2016: Cops become Evil, Threats, and Targets of Terror

↓ ↑

2012 - Present Black youth are terrified

2009 - Present Attitude of unkindness, disrespect, and hatred is sanctioned: *(Ex: Political Disrespect/Donald Trump/**Trump-Terror**, Non-teaching of cursive writing, No Sight-sight reading Music Notations, Social Media Disrespect, Students passing tests but learning nothing))*

2015-2016: Helpless, Hopelessness, Apathy sets in Black youth
(They are going to kill us anyway!)
2016: Terrorized objects of revenge become terrors
2016: Authority Figures (Cops) become evil, targets of revenge.
(The Law wasn't made to help Blacks attitude in Blacks)
2016: Killing of Cops by Blacks Sons
Everything White (White establishment) is a Nigger too =
The law wasn't made for us and will kill us anyway;
so we will kill them before they kill us.

TERROR RETURNED FROM BLACKS
↓
THE BLACK-WHITE AMERICAN DIVIDE

WELCOME TO THE WILD-WILD WEST AMERICA!

We know that blacks are unjustly killed by white police officers (who are supposed to be our protectors). As reported in the Washington Post, *"However, black men accounted for 40 percent of the 60 unarmed deaths, even though they make up just 6 percent of the U.S. population. The Post's analysis shows that black men were seven times more likely than white men to die by police gunfire while unarmed."*[8]

Our sons and daughters are tired of being terrorized and are resorting to becoming terrors themselves. Though wrong, I understand this from personal experience. Thus, as emphasized, I wrote about *Roni* because, I experienced being terrorized to the point of becoming a Roni myself during my childhood, but I made the choice to not walk that way, although the temptation was overwhelming. Moreover, I am the mother of two lovely Black sons who could have become Ronies had I not prepared them to offset the perils of living "black" in America. So I taught them how to act and this was accomplished by teaching

---

[8] Retrieved from: http://www.washingtonpost.com/sf/national/2015/08/08/black-and-unarmed/?tid=a_inl; on July 11, 2016.

them to act right. Therefore, I love Roni because I love myself and I love my black sons. I taught my sons how to act by teaching and showing them good manners and good Christ-followership. Training our children as they should go is our best safeguard against them being mistreated.

I choose not to demonstrate Roni because I learned how I should act from my Big Mama and from the Bible. Then I taught my sons how to act from what I learned. I do this because "Acting-right" works best in every situation. In other words, we do not have to act like someone we've been fashioned to become. We can become all we should be by the God-given power of choice. This power is within all of us but it's up to YOU! We are free to choose and to choose without regret. Then when it's all said and done, we can have peace about how our lives have gone. Overall, I want Roni to be free to be the best he or she can become without the hidden influences of Roni-making. Thus, I want to demonstrate God's love to Roni since those being injured and killed could be me or my black sons

> THOSE YOU TERRORIZE WILL EVENTUALLY TERRORIZE YOU!

See other stats on the killings of blacks by police on the following page.

WHY TEACH RONI?

We should teach Roni because he lacks the power of knowledge. If I fail to teach Roni, I am turning my back upon myself; someone taught me and didn't leave me behind when I needed a teacher. Thus I must try to awaken my own people to God by teaching them. When I learned better I could do better and so can Roni. Knowledge is hidden from those who are unlearned and from those who are ignorant. There is a difference between an unlearned person and an ignorant person. Yet, everyone deserves a chance to learn.

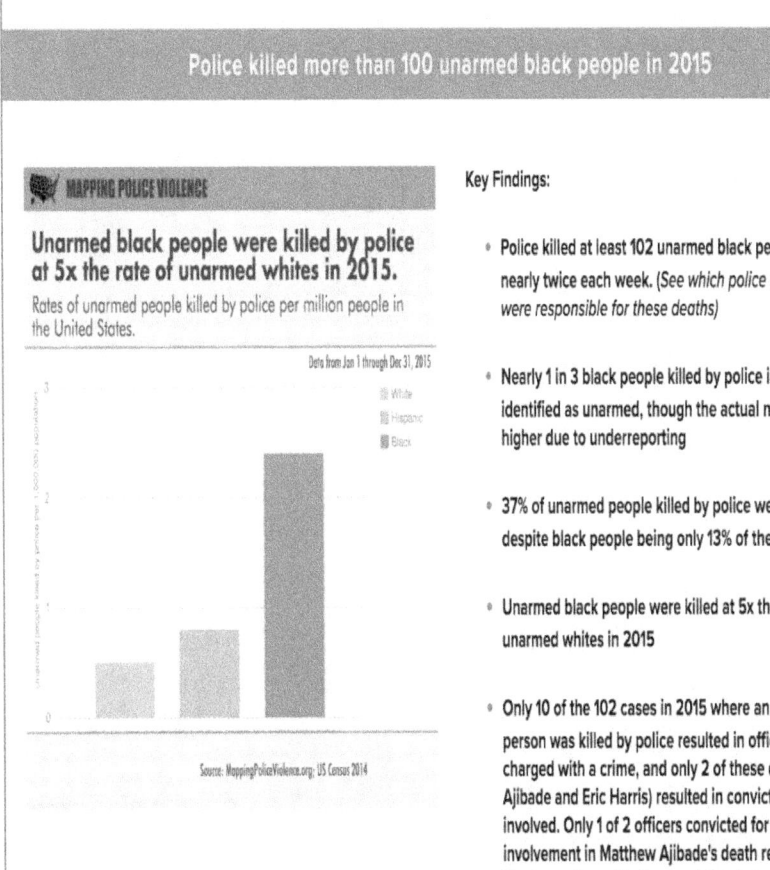

[Taken from: http://mappingpoliceviolence.org/unarmed/].

UNLEARNED: He has not been taught and shown and he is willing, to learn but is unable because he does not know that:
1. He does not have knowledge because he/she **has not learned.**
2. He **does not have a teacher** or does not know he/she has a teacher.

3. He **does not understand an instruction** for the subject matter.
4. He has **not had an opportunity** to learn so he does not know.

IGNORANT: He has been taught and shown and he is able, but is unwilling because he will not obey what he knows because:
1. His conscience is hardened (1 Timothy 4:2)
2. Satan has blinded his eyes; (2 Corinthians 4:4)
3. He is not of God (John 8:47)
4. He sees what is right in their own way, does not see the right way (Proverbs 14:12)
5. He is a fool (Ecclesiastes 10:2)
6. He does not love oneself (Proverbs 19:8)
7. He chooses not to hear (Proverbs 20:12; Revelation 2: 7, 29)

Ultimately the difference between an unlearned person and an ignorant person is that of a righteous person and an unrighteous person since we cannot live what we do not know.

Unawareness of the law does not exonerate us from the injustice or penalty of the law!

UNLEARNED: Does not know a bottomless hole is in the road so he falls in the hole.

IGNORANT: Knows there is a bottomless hole in the road, but falls in the hole regardless.

IGNORANT *AND* UNLEARNED?

An unlearned or unaware righteous person has not had an opportunity to learn; so he does not know or has not been given instruction. For example, a driver is speeding because the speeding limit sign is blocked by a tree and the driver is unaware of the speeding limit. The driver gets a speeding ticket, but shows the court that the sign was not visible. The ticket is thus dismissed, but the driver owns his mistakes and seeks to know the speed limit to prevent future speeding tickets. Here the driver is unaware of the speeding limit, but seeks to know and thereafter acts accordingly and does not exceed the speed limit.

The ignorant or willfully wrong unrighteous person knows what is right, but turns against "right" despite his/her knowledge. He/she hears, but ignores the voice of reason and is willfully disobedient. For example, a driver sees the posted speed limit sign, but chooses to ignore it and gets a speeding ticket. Then he refuses to own that he ignored the sign while seeking to blame someone or something outside of himself for the ticket. Here, the driver is aware of the speeding limit but refuses to obey what he knows. Further proving his ignorance, he does not accept responsibility for getting the ticket. Roni fails to do what he/she knows to do and most often fall into the category of an ignorant person.

Sadly, however, Roni is both ignorant and unlearned resulting in a *certain person* who: (1) Does not know; (2) Does not want to know; (3) Doesn't know he does not know.

IS TEACHING RONI A WASTE OF TIME?

Regardless of the seeming futility of teaching Roni, the answer to the above question is "No." Teaching helps and helping others is never a waste of time. I'm not expecting immediate results. I'm doing the work and leaving the results up to God. Those of us who know are accountable and should teach those who do not know and we must re-teach those who refuse to do what they *do* know. We are to *teach them* anyway because it is God who gives the results. Teach and leave the results up to God because we can't help those who will not receive help; but we can try and perhaps save more of the same group.

One waters, one plants, but God brings the increase. Since God is sovereign we must trust Him with the results and leave the results up to Him. I might be undertaking a futile project by writing this book, but at least I am trying to get more of the "some" who might want to know. I will teach and leave the results up to God. I am open to evaluating my presentation, my effectiveness, how I am able to speak truth in love, if I am befitting my audience, and the readiness to learn of those I am teaching, but I still believe I should try to reach everyone. We, who have learned, are to teach *what is right* and *what is wrong*, to everyone, although I know we can't save everyone. Yet, we must teach in a way that does not immobilize people to a point that keeps Roni from moving forward. And don't be offended by my candid approach, but if you are offended remember, I said "some are not all," 'cause, "A hit dog will holler!" So, please so lease hear my heart?

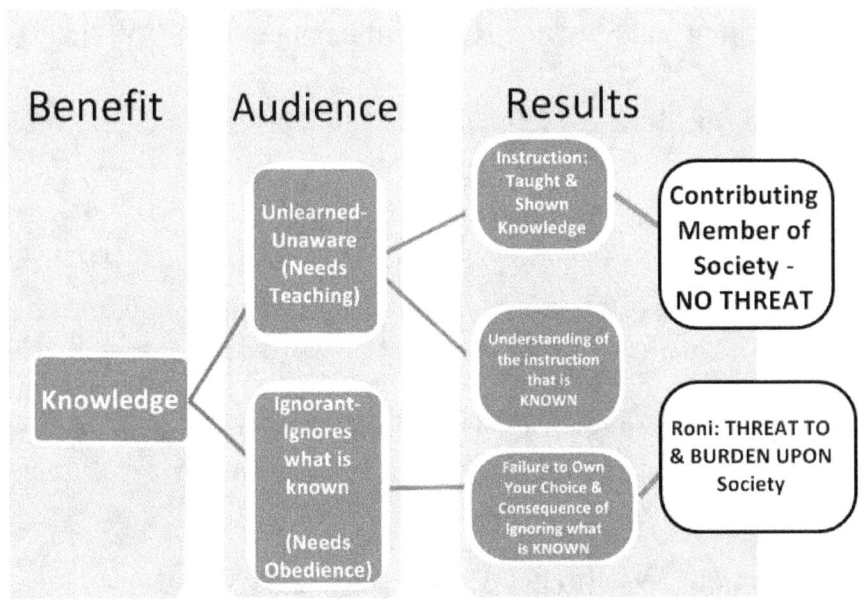

SO WHY AM I TRYING TO TEACH RONI?

I am trying to teach Roni because:

- No one is teaching Roni what Roni basically needs to know, i.e., Six Simple Lessons, that we all know to give us safety and success; instead everyone is helping Roni to make excuses.
- When I see Roni I see myself and since I love myself and my black sons, I want to share what I have learned.
- What is happening to Roni in America could have happened to my sons or to me, had we not been taught how to overcome Roni.
- Roni has not been taught and shown,
- Roni knows but refuses to obey what he knows, and
- Roni will have a chance to obey what he knows if he is taught and shown,

- Teaching and Showing Roni will demonstrate LOVE to Roni,
- Everyone deserves KINDNESS and RESPECT, even Roni!

MY PERSONAL EXPERIENCE WITH RACIST TERRORISM

"The law wasn't made to help no little nigger bitches, and if anybody is mistreating you, that's what you deserve!" The deputy spat at me when he did not believe I had a valid handicapped parking permit. What follows is the account, written as a letter to the peace officer who showed me what racist terrorism looks like up close and personal.

To the bully-sheriff who treated as if I am a N–

First of all, you let me see firsthand how abusive authority figures like you have created a racist war in America between those of different appearances—The Black-White American Divide. I am a law-abiding, tax-paying, contributor to society—citizen. I am not a nigger (one without respect or care for myself and others), yet you treated me like I am nothing and as if my life, my dignity, and self-esteem do not matter. You were out of line publicly terrorizing me and this is not your job. People like you saying, "I'm just doing my job," have caused racial tension that has led to all this race-killing in America. And it is all because of those with the white supremacists attitude. Although you are Hispanic, you have this attitude, you have created terror, and you need to know, *Black is one thing and N– is another. Everything Black is not a nigger.*

Just because I'm Black doesn't mean I'm a nigger trying to get over on society. It is not your job to abuse your authority and make yourself judge and jury, especially when you have wrongly judged. I don't have to LOOK handicapped and you should know that disabled license plates and placards are registered with the state and can be verified by you, as a lawman. When you hate people without a cause—as you demonstrated to me—you can't do anything but attack and kill them. You caused me to regress back to a terrorized teenager seeking help from an uncaring legal system with bully-cops like you, "doing their jobs".

This is what you said about yourself when you terrorized me working as a security guard working for Chick-Fil-A, a so-called Christian organization. You make the law, the church, and God look bad because you are a N– too (disrespecting a citizen and yourself). I am going to do what I can to regain the respect you took from me by using Caesar's resources, and writing about you in this book. What the devil meant for evil is working for my good because I had to relive the trauma you triggered so that I could release it and improve the quality of my life. Moreover, I see what people like you have done to hurt society in the name of Christ and the law; but where has that gotten us? Your kind (racist) has divided us and now you are targets of the wrongful collateral damage you have created! Shame on you bully-lawman, for wronging me and wrongdoing society.

Whereas, I will use the nonviolent approach to fighting against your kind of injustice and seek justice through the legal system, this generation doesn't care about nonviolence, thinking you are going to kill them anyway and they are willing to die to fight against your brutality. You have torn down what you should build-up—America. Now your kind is getting back what you have dished out. Two wrongs don't make a right, but as my son would say to his brother when he was about to get punished for hitting him, "You started it!"

Shame on you, Deputy and Chick-Fil-A of Missouri City, Texas, for allowing this bully (so-called) peace officer to treat me this way, with both of you saying he was doing his job. How is doing your job the wrong way, working for us? So you seem to think the same way as those engaged in the hunting season on Blacks in America right now who think meaning no harm while doing harm and while you are killing us, is "doing your jobs." I'm taking you to court but most people won't.

I believe you know protocol, but chose not to follow it with me because I am a black female who you thought did not deserve to have a handicap placard. Who qualified you to determine what a disabled person looks like? And how it is protocol to justify wronging people by saying you're doing you're jobs when you are doing your job wrongly? Protocol is doing the job the right way, ok? Or did you decide to change the protocol because I did not look disabled as a black female? Changing the protocols by color is wrong and is not working so good for America right now is it? As a peace officer, you are to treat all people with equal regard, but you did not follow your own protocol. I believe you did not treat me with the protocol because you considered me as an N-word. But as I stated, Black is one thing and Nword is another, and sadly you don't know that you're a Nword yourself, to have disrespected me on the basis of my appearance.

I am not a Nword; I am a citizen. So I'm taking this matter to court, whereas many are taking it to the streets! Treating citizens like Nwords is not working in America. Why? Because when you nullify the existence of people (in your mind), violence is inevitable. All lives matter!

Wrongful Collateral Damage

After experiencing this traumatizing incident wherein a so-called law enforcement officer, harassed, threatened, and accosted me, I understood how law enforcement racially profiles, stereotypes, discriminates against and commits brutality against us. This sheriff thought I was illegally parked. Consequently he treated me like a Roni, trying to "get one over" when I was within my legal rights—I was not illegally parked. It was from this incident that I gained an understanding of the big picture of dual injustice—Racism & Ronism. I wrote this book to decrease and hopefully eliminate Roni-making by Ronies in charge which leads to the prejudicial discrimination of Black people. Discrimination is mistreatment while prejudice is a mental position. In other words, just because someone is prejudiced, doesn't mean they have to discriminate against someone else.

Prejudice is an attitude while discrimination is an act. We can make it less likely for *bully-cops* to injure or kill us by making sure that we are not alarming people or looking like a threat to society. The legal system is not going to punish *them* for this type of behavior because they believe this is the price we must pay for freedom and safety and that they are just doing their jobs. This is referred to as *Collateral Damage*. Collateral Damage is by definition unintended injuries, damage, or death through action, but *bully-cops* commit this as *Wrongful Collateral Damage* because their biases cause them to act with intent to injure, damage, and kill through their actions.

I want to put a stop to Wrongful Collateral Damage as I feared would happen to me when the bully-lawman wearing a badge and a gun could have killed me—I feared for my life. I knew if he did kill me, no one would do anything about it, because I remember how they killed Ida Delaney (10/31/1989) and got away with it and I see how it happens nowadays to our black men. When they kill you, they just look into your history to find some justification to have done it; so it's best to stay out of

39

their way. These kinds of Zimmerman's and bully-cops need to know, "Don't terrify and kill children and law-abiding citizens— correct and shield them!" But they are too paranoid, hateful, and threatened to think rationally.

DON'T TERRIFY AND KILL—CORRECT AND SHIELD

Had I made a wrong move, I would have been a victim of *Wrongful Collateral Damage*. His biases were provoking him to act against me although I presented no provocation to him. He terrified me looking at me and talking to me like I was an NWord!

I didn't react or retaliate because I have learned not to escalate in stressful situations. I didn't resist him or challenge him; I was afraid of him. So, I called the *police* on the *police* (I called 911).

Bully-cops believe that all Black people are Roni's and Black people think that all cops are bully-cops. But just like Roni, *some* does not mean *all* and *most* does not mean *all*. We know it's never *all*, but when there are so many that make it lop-sided, it looks like it's *all*. This applies to both sides of the coin.

Poor things, these bully-lawmen don't know they are Ronies, too. I

> NO MATTER WHAT, WE DO NOT DESERVE TO BE TERRORIZED, BEATEN, OR MASSACRED.

know we must hold Roni at bay, but injustice is not the way to succeed. We must *teach* Roni and *not kill* Roni. No matter what, we do not deserve to be terrorized, beaten, or massacred.

When I called the police on this bully-cop, the dispatcher said this was not a life-threatening situation, but I said, "I fear for my life because this man is in a rage with a gun and won't even hear that he is free to run my *Disabled State Registered License Plate*," yelling, "What's wrong with you?! You don't look like anything is wrong with you; you are violating the law and I'm tired of *you*-people parking here that don't belong to you; you can't use your mother's placard...and on and on." He wrote down my license plate to issue me a ticket and although he worked for Chick-Fil-A, the manager would take no action to stop his brutality, so I had to call the police on the sheriff.

When I called the police, I told the dispatcher that this was a life-threatening situation *to me* and insisted that officers with some sense be dispatched who would be reasonable and not in a rage with a gun, further saying to the dispatcher, "White policemen kill Black folks and disabled people all the time, and get away with it, and I don't want to be a casualty of this nonsense."

So, two *non-Roni* police officers were dispatched; they understood that I had been wronged, communicated this to the bully-sheriff, reported the incident to the bully-sheriff's superior, and told me that I was free to leave the scene, which you should never do until released. Never, ever leave the scene until it has been officially resolved because if you leave the story will change and everything will fall against you. Fortunately, I got some law-abiding-lawmen who deescalated the situation and released me from the scene.

I was abiding by the law. So I avoided the *injustice* of the law by *obeying* the law. This is *injustice avoidance*. I was not doing anything wrong, but the sheriff still treated me like I was doing wrong, because he stereotyped me, obviously perceiving me as a Roni and Chick-Fil-A's manager said, "I can't do anything about him because he is the police doing his job." So, she failed to protect me from this abuser and allowed him to cause me anguish.

Isn't that something? He was doing *his* job and doing the *wrong* thing and he was celebrated, while I was doing my job at the Houston VA Medical Center doing the *right* thing (as an educated black woman, doing my job) and I was desecrated.

41

This is a mixed bag of rules wherein White folks[9] are given a different set of rules and for the same right or wrong behavior. While we are punished for *right* behavior, White-folks doing the same or opposite from what is right, are rewarded. For example when we are absent because we are sick, they think of us just not wanting to work; and when White-folks are absent because they are sick, they are really sick—same behavior treated differently. We need same behavior, same treatment, but for us we suffer under the injustice of a mixed bag of rules. Thus, we must do better, be better, and act better to get the same or lesser treatment. At any rate, acting right will put us in better standing to receive better treatment; moreover, we receive God's favor against injustice.

MIXED BAG OF RULES FOR US?

I suffered this mixed bag of rules by the bully-cop because he saw me as a nigger although I did not show myself to be a nigger. Just doing his job, huh? So, *if* he would have killed me "doing his job" in his prejudicial rage, neither he nor Chick-Fil-A would have taken any accountability for my death because they considered the sheriff—who worked for them—"as doing his job." He was breaking the law, harassing, terrorizing, profiling and discriminating against me, and exposing me to danger through Wrongful Collateral Damage. His behavior demonstrated White Supremacy although he was Mexican/Hispanic.

PROVOKED BY HIS OWN PREJUDICE

In this White Supremacy mindset were: 1. The belief that he was superior to me and should dominate over me; 2. A generalized hatred of me; 3. Mistreatment of me due to his belief

---

[9](by the way Hispanic is an ethnic identity and can be of any racial group--Yellow, Red, Black, White, or Brown, but most of them think they are better than (superior to) Black folks and act like they think they are White-folks with the feeling that we are beneath them and they are superior to us just like White-folks and Africans who are the worst acting toward US)

in his own superiority and his hatred that took my worth to zero and gave him justification to abuse and/or kill me. These ideas are expressed through white supremacy. If the sheriff security officer would have killed me it would have been for *nothing* because "white supremacy" is accepted in the minds of the public. People were passing by saying and doing nothing and the manager of Chick-fil-a said she could do *nothing* to stop him from discriminating against me because she said, "He is only doing his job."

Was he doing his job by racially profiling, stereotyping and discriminating against me? And Chick-fil-a is supposed to be a Christian organization? So it goes for Christians—doing wrong and calling it right. I thought I was going to die that day because of the color of my skin—because a bully-cop believed that all Black people should be eliminated because we are all NWords.

Sadly, white folks love animals and treat them better than they treat black people. They even think enough of a dog to give them healthcare insurance and medical care when they don't think enough of a black person to care if we have health insurance. Innocent young hopefuls for a bright future are subject to racial cruelty as well. I am a professional and this so-called lawman terrorized me into a panic attack. God only knows how he'd affect a unsuspecting young person.

> THE LOPSIDED APPEARANCE OF **ALL** RESULTS IN WRONGFUL COLLATERAL DAMAGE, BUT **SOME** DOES NOT MEAN **ALL;** **ONE** DOES NOT MEAN **ALL;** AND **MOST** DOES NOT MEAN **ALL.**

If I would have provoked this sheriff in some way—in the least bit, God only knows how he could have been *trigger happy* and shot me; then they could justify killing me by looking into my history and saying, "She was either colored, crazy, or a criminal, "saying he was just doing his job. The cops killing us wrongly are using this same excuse; but is, terrorizing and murdering us, doing their jobs? As a result of my traumatic childhood I have a mental health history and people wrongly write us off as crazy and give us absolutely no respect or common courtesy. But the "crazy" justification is the oldest trick in the book, but it still works because there is a general disrespect for citizens with mental health challenges, although we do not commit a majority of the crime and have not self-inflicted our conditions. Because he saw me as an N-Word trying to get one over, he treated me that way when I was not doing anything wrong and offering him to match my driver's license with my number on the State of Texas registered disability placard. He doesn't know that "because someone is Black, doesn't mean they are an N-Word."

So, Don't treat me like I'm a nigger because I am not one!

COMPONENTS OF RACISM AGAINST ALL BLACKS:

Wrongful Collateral Damage together with Racist Terrorism is a two-way street of:

1. **Known and Unknown Bias and Hatred by Haters, Abusive Authority Figures/Cops**: Racial and cultural biases in awareness and unawareness in ignorant people with authority like police-bullies with badges and guns; and vigilante citizens who are NWords themselves of all colors and kinds dish out racist terrorism disguised as doing their jobs and business as usual;

2. **The Lopsided Effect by the misrepresentation of Blacks by NWords**: Disproportionate numbers of bad-actors within a cultural group that feeds into an *appearance of all* bias and hatred in fools who believe that the lopsided *some* means *all,* that results in fools hating the *all* without just cause; this brings about wrongful collateral damage and terrorism against Black people. I

know that everyone and every group has some bad-acting going on, but to me, we're the most and the worst of the bad-actors; so we get the worst treatment. We are gifted in everything, good or bad. So, we look lopsided.

I conducted a convenient sample of respondents across the US and the survey results were that every group has bad-actors but the worst of the bad actors seem to be Black people; the study has not been put thru empirical methods therefore it stands as a theory, perception or connotation. However, since connotation, perception and theories are beliefs that are not necessarily accurate, people still treat them as if they are accurate. Thus it doesn't matter if they are accurate or not if they are treated as if they are valid. Yet, this *appearance of all* does not justify killing, injuring, and terrorizing us. The lopsided effect is a deception but is not treated as deception, rather treated as if it is real and we all suffer for it. The lopsided appearance of all results in wrongful collateral damage. But *some* does not mean *all*; *one* does not mean *all*; and *most* does not mean *all.*

Fortunately, because, I was *in* the right and *did* right, I did not put myself in a position to be discredited, harmed, or killed by this bully-cop. I made it less likely for this fool with a gun to kill me. This is the main lesson Roni must learn—don't give them a reason, because although I know there is a difference between Black and nigger, many White people don't know this. They think anything Black is a nigger, but everything that is Black is not a nigger; some cows are black, are those niggers? If a horse is black, is that a nigger? Is a black dog a nigger? Get my drift?

Yes, when you are a part of Black American Society most White-folks will always consider you as Roni, like my grandmother taught me. We will be the last hired, first fired, will have to do more to get less or the same, and will receive the maximum penalty in a White man's court. Sadly, many of us think *Black* means nigger too and we have allowed the

45

interchange of Black to mean nigger and nigger to mean Black, but Black is one thing and nigger is another, because niggers come in all colors, not just Black. There are White niggers, Brown niggers, Yellow niggers, Red niggers, as well as Black niggers. So the question remains, "Why are we the worse off, having some of the best at everything among us, even bad-acting? I believe we are worst off because we won't do the right thing by ourselves, others, and God. Now it has gotten so bad that we all suffer for the wrongdoing and bad-acting that Roni is doing. So many Ronies act so bad so well until we and White-folks don't know the difference between what is Black and what is Roni. This results in an interchangeable misnomer that causes everything black to be treated like niggers. But I am asking White folks: *don't treat me like I'm a nigger until I show you I'm a nigger!*

Black Americans have core values and these are not White or NWord values. We do have core values. Big Mama taught me these values and we lived in a segregated community; so these values are not "White." We have values too, such as:

Black Core Value	Reason 4 the Value	Vs. NWord Core Values
1. To Work	An idle mind is the devil's workshop	Don't want to or have to work because I can beg, borrow, and still yo stuff, especially TV's
2. To be pure	If you lie with dogs, you will get fleas	I do whatever I feel like doing with anyone I want to do it with (sleeping around)

3. Don't lie	If you lie, you will steal and if you steal you will kill.	Everybody lies; so it must be OK since everybody does it.
4. To keep your word	Your word is your bond; so keep your promises and pay your bills to have a good name	I don't care about breaking a promises because I make them to break them.
5. To have a good name	A good name is better than great riches	I don't care about what people think, even when I cause them to think it (something bad)
6. Respect your elders	You're gonna obey somebody; even if you learn this in jail because we are to obey those who have rule over us and honor our parents/elders.	Can't nobody tell me what to do!
7. Respect for the Laws of the land	If you go to jail, don't call me cause, I'm not paying one penny for you to get out.	I won't get caught; and if I do get caught, "so what."
8 Obey the Golden Rule: Treat others as yourself	What you do comes back to you and when you dig one ditch you might as well dig two (one for yourself).	I don't care for anybody but myself and I'll get them before they get me cause they're going to get me anyway.

9. Respect for modesty	If you aint't for sale take down your sign. "Cover yourself up in front of menfolks and keep him from sinning, cause men's is dogs."	So what if I show my nakedness to the world; it's my body and I can show it to anybody I want to; privacy doesn't matter, not even my private matters; because I give it away to any and everybody.
10. Respect for keeping still/sitting still	"Go sit down somewhere!" "Keep yourself still!" You can't learn or look like you have any sense if you can't keep still. Twitching, jerking, pointing, shaking, showing a bad attitude, and moving to the wrong person (bully cop) can get you killed!	"Children will be children." "Men will be men." "Girls will be girls," meaning people are excused to act any kind of way.
11. Obeying authority figures	You're gonna hear somebody! If you won't hear me, you will hear in the penitentiary.	You can't tell me what to do, even when you are in charge, even when I work for you, and even when I am living in your house.

12. Respect for Marriage	If she's/he's good enough to lay with you; he/she is good enough for you to pay the price and marry her/him.	I want the pleasure of marriage but not the responsibility of it. I fool around with any and everybody I see; whenever I feel like it and it doesn't matter if we are married in or out of the church.

These are the values we learned and we can lessen our chances of being treated like a nigger by doing what we culturally value and have been taught to do that is right. Just because White-folks are trying to catch us and put us down, doesn't mean we have to walk into their trap; so don't blame the trap; take responsibility for stepping into it. Yet, killing me is not okay, even if my name is Roni. All lives matter, including Roni's life.

So don't act out against Ronies of any kind (bully-cops, racists, bullies, scorners, or bigots). Take them to Caesar (the law) and let it work for you. I've been successful allowing Caesar to help me with Ronies and keep trash off my hands!

Chapter 3   The Roni Test

How Do I Know I'm Roni?

If this sounds like you, then you're a Roni. Just take the test and admit all that apply to you by saying I am Roni because I:

1. **DISREGARD FOR DOING RIGHT**:
   I know what is right, but refuse to do what is right. Then, I expect good consequences from making bad choices; so I never look at myself or learn from what I have caused in my life; I look at what THEY are doing NOT at what I am doing or have done.

2. **DISREGARD FOR THE PERSONAL BOUNDARIES AND THE PERSONAL AUTHORITY OF OTHERS**:
   Thus, I'm always running or trying to run things, persons, and places that I am not in charge of. I am controlling, nosey, meddling, and a busybody; thus, I suffer as a murderer, a thief, and a busybody because I take the joy, lives, possessions, and/or authority of others, instead of attending to my own life/affairs. I suffer for being a meddler but never realize I cause my own suffering. Rather than learning to attend to my own needs/business from those who attend their own affairs I hate-on them especially when they won't let me benefit from what they've accomplished, by attending to their own business/affairs.

3. **A NOISE POLLUTION-MAKER**:

   I think everybody wants to hear my deafening base-booming music and conversations (on the cell phone, between me and someone else, etc); so I'm always too loud. This also applies to Mexicans/Latinos who blast neighbors with loud fiesta music that annoys everyone. I have no respect for other folk's ears or personal space; I create noise pollution!

4. **POOR/NO PARENTING SKILLS:**

   I try to raise my children in public or not at all in the privacy of my home and do nothing in public when they tear up and touch things that do not belong to them. I don't want anyone to correct my child and I don't correct them either; so I spoil my kids and leave them to ruin.

5. **UNACCOUNTABLE (to anyone) FOR WHAT I THINK, LOOK LIKE or ACT LIKE:**

   Thus I am bad mannered, ignorant, and unmanageable. I don't know good manners and don't think they're important; so I am a bad person even when I say I am a Christian, devout person, or person of faith.

6. **DRESS INAPPROPRIATELY:**

   I don't know when and where to wear at home clothing or where to show my nakedness so I expose myself in the wrong places and look like I have no self-respect because I think life is a beach.

7. **DISREGARD FOR RULES:**

   I won't follow the rules unless I am forced and I think this way because I think rules are good only when someone doesn't follow them with me; otherwise, rules are not real and mean nothing to me; so I have no personal boundaries or standards.

8. **DISRESPECT FOR LEADERSHIP:**

I discount exemplary people and call them ugly names (especially calling them crazy/stupid) to discredit them, especially if they require me to do things the right way; so I can never benefit from greatness around me.

9. **AN UNTRUSTWORTHY BORROWER:**

I think people owe me something; so I feel perfectly okay borrowing money that I will not/cannot pay back and am all right asking people to do for me what I can do for myself because I think they *owe* me to do this; I am untrustworthy and if you loan me money or extend credit to me, I won't pay you or pay you back.

10. **A WORK SHIRKER:**

I'm able-bodied, but don't want to work because I can always try to "get one over" on somebody else; so I'm lazy and irresponsible but won't admit it. I have a bad-attitude with people an am unresponsive at work because I don't want to work.

11. **DISRESPECT FOR AUTHORITY INCLUDING DISRESPECT FOR GOD:**

Thus, I'm always out-of-order because 1 have no respect for God, others, myself or the law authority except for when I'm in front of the police or a judge which are the only places I know how to act; so I don't know how to act, cannot be courteous, and cannot see what I can and cannot change., otherwise. I do nothing to make myself socially, secularly, spiritually, sexually, and financially mature and independent; I am rude and feel good about myself although I do not have proper relationships with other people or with God (horizontal and vertical balance). I am extremely religious but unspiritual and demonstrate no relationship with God as demonstrated in my conduct.

12. **IN DENIAL ABOUT MY BAD CHARACTER AND CONDUCT:**
I deny that I am Roni; so that I can't ever learn anything that will help me to improve my situation. I am merely blowing in the wind and never enjoying the breeze.

Like I said, affectionately my name is Roni, short for the N-Word. I come in all colors—Yellow, Red, Brown, Black and White. I come in all kinds, and I come in all shapes and sizes and I am in all places. This means I am not about a LOOK, but about an ACT. Many Black-Ronies don't know they are Ronies, but many White-Ronies don't know that they are Ronies, too, because anybody can be Roni!

REJECTED BY MY OWN SKIN

After my motherland rejected me and sold me out, I was lost and away from home, forced to live in America and was taught everything that I know to do wrong by white folks because I forgot my own values. So, I obtained and insulting name (N........) long, long ago, back and forth ever since. Now America is split right down the middle between black and white. And we've not admitted or corrected anything that we have done against ourselves or that they have done against us since our history began. We would not be terrorized of the thought of someone sending us "BACK" to someplace where we do not belong, and did not come from in the first place, if we understood our identity—American everything and African nothing. But zeroed-out folks are always running to what we are running from, looking for love and acceptance in all the wrong places. Only until we know who we are, will be understand that "You can't send someone back to somewhere they were never from!"

Let me point out a shocker about African-Ronies. We need not be fooled by those from our rejecting motherland. Many of them are the worst of all colored folks and they treat us worse than White folks ever have—Africans seem to hate us anyway—too often they think they are better than us just like white folks and consequently they disrespect us too. They hate us in the country we were born in, for no reason. They overlook us when we are standing in line shopping, and just break the lines without regard for us standing there—right in their faces. They are the rudest of all people who suck up to White folks and treat us like crap. They engage in all kinds of schemes and illegal activity and can run back to their country after they ruin our careers with their schemes. You won't do business with them if you know what's good for you. Thank God they're not in charge in America! They sold us into slavery in the first place, and have never done anything for us or their own kind. Guess it's not surprising that they'd be so hateful when they are a tribal country divided against themselves, destined to fall. A friend said to me that Nigeria has a myriad of tribes in a land smaller than one of our 50 states. We are worse on ourselves than our oppressors. Africa is oppressive to women, diseased, and in abject poverty. They are a divided people who disrespect us and we have the nerve to let society call us African-Americans?

GETTING THE RIGHT NAME

I'm not an African of any kind: American, German, Italian, or Mexican. I am ONLY American! We are American and that's all; not an African anything! So we need to fix our name and fix our identity.

We are not African of any kind and have no reason to have African pride, especially with the shape Africa is in with oppressive leaders. Africa is an example of the kind of internal harm we can do to one another—harm that White people have nothing to do with. Who has messed up Africa? Africans! Just like what messed up Roni. Ronies! We mess ourselves up because we are so shameful, licentious, rude, selfish, sinful, wicked, and sexually impure. We didn't learn, "If you lay with dogs you will end up with flees." We are always wanting to be sexual when we need to be ethical, always wanting to be insulting when we need to be polite, trying to be sexy when we need to demonstrate modesty—even our so-called pastors, missionaries, and community leaders, trying to be funny when we need to be serious, trying to be naked when we need to be covered up, and reading each other when we need to be reading a book.

I can't stand *our* pompous, prideful and disrespectful Ronies of all kinds, always sexy, loud, lying, butts all out, cheating, using, and looking down on each other. At least when Black folk were freed from African enslavement, America offered them the freedom of Jesus, but it was African people who enslaved Black folk in Africa and in America. So though freed we cannot benefit from what Jesus has to offer us because Roni-preachers point us to themselves instead of to God. Sadly, we just follow along like we're stupid. I don't understand why we won't just know God and read the Bible for ourselves and stop looking for a human to lead us to God. We want idols not individuation. And Jesus is not a white man or a black preacher!

CHURCH SLAVES?

If you want to know what's wrong with the Black race, look at what's wrong with the Black church! Making Us *Poor In Character* and *Poor In Cash*.

Slave-owner-Ronies started off saying, "The Roni's can't read." They still say that we don't and cannot read. I hope we will read what I am saying about us, so we can make good choices for Roni and not let Roni make choices for us. We must say, "I'm in charge of Roni and Roni is not in charge of me!"

I was started by those who do not look like me, but mass-produced by those who do look like me. Wow, how did that happen? Well, the Ronies took the place of slave-owners and started mass-producing me. So, Ronies and non-Ronies benefit from my mass-production, but I am now mass-produced by Ronies. And guess what? This mass-production of Roni has nothing to do with White Folks, although White-folks take advantage of the results of Roni-making by Ronies.

How is Roni Produced?

I was manufactured by those in so-called "church leadership" who look like me. And we have the nerve to blame White folks? White folks don't have anything to do with Ronies making Ronies out of us, especially in the church. This is the all-time exclusive Black Production and the replacement of 19th Century Slavery—Ronies making Ronies. Pastor = Master or Massa.

The New Slavery? Pastors in the Roni church are our slave masters who live above us on *our* means as if they are kings when they are so needy and greedy that they can't even tell us the truth. And is this supposed to be a church? I don't know what church this is because God

> PASTORS IN THE RONI CHURCH ARE SLAVE MASTERS WHO LIVE ABOVE US ON **OUR** MEANS.

sho ain't in this Roni mess called a church. It's pitiful that church Ronies aren't doing anything to build up the kingdom for the King, and not build up Roni-dom for Roni-pastors to be kings over slaves they've made of their own people. Poor kings who depend on the people's money?

Brothers and sisters, we *can* build up the kingdom for the King, and not to build up Roni-dom for the sole benefit of the Roni-preachers, Roni-church, Hollywood, the legal system, and the State prison system. And please know that the State and the

Church are married and are working together against Roni.

Unfortunately, the church raises up criminals and bad-actors for the state to lock up since it is where most Ronies congregate. Thus, it is in the best position to make Roni smaller, but it fails to do so. The two main problems with the Roni-Church making Roni skinny are:

1. Broke and Bad-acting Dumb-Roni-Preachers; and 2. Broke and Bad-acting Ronies. We cannot teach what we don't know; cannot teach what we refuse to teach that we do know; and we can't lead where we do not go. Nor can we make good Christians out of bad-actors. First, you make them good people or law-abiding citizens, then you can instill Christian behavior.

Contrarily, in the Roni-church you have dumb-Roni-preachers who are trying to make good Christians out of bad-actors and that won't work. Our Head "N's" In Charge (HNICs) train us to have no character and no money telling us that *God is going to fix our mess-ups and that God is going to do what we are supposed to do for ourselves.* How is it working that God is going to fix it?

Missing In Action (MIA) Spirituality

We act as if we are pimping God, using him to get what we want, but show no reverence to Him in our daily lives. And we wonder why our pockets are running on empty? Our Roni-preachers don't understand that, "You cannot be dependent upon people and lead them at the same time." They teach us to *poor mouth* because *they ain't got no money,* except what they can trick us out of, in God's name. If they had anything to offer other than feeding us the same meal all the time, their gifts would make room for them. But some were called and some went, but most of them have not been sent. Because they have not been called by God, they make slaves of us to keep us more frightened, more guilt-ridden, poorer, and more ignorant than they are in order to make a living doing what they were not called to do.

When Roni-preachers huff and puff about the Bible, they only rehash the same old stories about Peter and John, but never tell us about me and you. So, we sit up either looking stupid because we *don't know why* they are talking about what they are talking about, *or* we look like we are interested and *don't know what* they are talking about. If they didn't make us feel scared to death about hell and guilty as heck about ourselves, they would have no way to keep us enslaved—by the same old predictable stories.

> AIN'T NOBODY USING THEIR OWN AUTHORITY WHEN THEY'RE SPEAKING GOD'S WORD, BECAUSE THE AUTHORITY BELONGS TO GOD.

We can't grow because Roni-preachers don't give us a diet to grow on. We can't go any further than our leaders because we don't know and won't go to a Bible School to learn how to be effective in what we do. We just like to hear ourselves talk, *even when we ain't sayin' nothin'*. The Roni-church is the only place where dumb-men folk-Ronies can go, put on a suit and be something when in the world they are nothing, but are trying to be big when little's already got them.

THE OPPRESSED, OPPRESSING WOMEN

Our menfolk abuse and use women in God's name and discriminate against our womenfolk just like the White folk discriminate against them. Unbelievable!

The men say we (women) can't be in charge of the church and do jobs like pastors and lead. They don't see that they are doing the same thing to women that White men are doing to us/them. We all open our big mouths talking about *who* God can use when God's word doesn't apply to a single person—His word applies to all of us. It is all about God's authority, not the men-folks or women-folks. *Ain't nobody using their own authority when they're speaking God's word because the authority belongs to God.* So what are men talking about that a woman cannot speak over a man because she cannot have authority over the man when the authority doesn't belong to a man or a woman, and nobody should put their own authority over another person unless they are a parent or boss? Menfolk think God's word is their authority when they are merely delegated, not discretionary; but since they think it's their authority they abuse it and attribute it to God.

Question is, "Whose authority is God's word anyway?" What are they talking about?

SEXISM = RACISM = TERRORISM

Our men don't really want freedom. They only want to be in the seat to oppress; so they oppress us—both our men and women. They de-masculinize real men; subordinate, abuse, exploit and assault women; and provoke, intimidate and demoralize children. That's why real men don't go to church, but weak women go, because that's where they can feel good about feeling that they are not worth very much. Children are forced to go by their parents, who go for social fellowship, but are not taught moral development due to the lack of teaching by skill or example. Then we can feel good about ourselves and stop bothering with everybody else. It is hell to live among nosey, uncaring, ungrateful, and hateful sideline judges all the time living with Roni

When men folks say, *"the women's is usurping her authority over the mens when she speaks God's words,"* they are not rightly dividing the Bible. This kind of talk makes no sense because it is ultimately God's authority. Who are they to say who God can use to speak His word or to lead people? Deborah,

Phoebe, Lydia and the women at the tomb spoke God's word and set an example for all women to lead. These Roni-men will never admit the truth because they want to control women in order to feel good about themselves—being nothing in the real world (the women run the church anyway). These Roni-men have no problem with women giving money and doing most of the work, but they want us to listen to their repeated overused stories and fall for their seduction because, *"they show ain't got no oil and no order."*

The only thing big about *us' men-folks and us' women-folks* is our big mouths, but we ain't gonna do nothing when it comes to putting some work to where our big mouth is. And, we ain't gonna do anything to make our so-called leaders be accountable to their callings.

> WHO ARE WE WORSHIPPING WHEN WE'RE DOING THE BUMP AND GRIND TO JESUS LYRICS?

We like being slaves, but problem is, slaves never can become kings while they are still slaves (Proverbs 30:22). Talk, talk, talk, talk, yet *ain't gonna do nothing* but hate on us who do put our mouths, money, and manpower together. We're always being envious and jealous when we could tend to our own business and get to work. Then we can feel good about ourselves and stop bothering with everybody else.

CHURCH OR NIGHT CLUB?

Much of Roni's so-called Gospel music is nothing but R&B, disrespectful to the Lord and much too sensual. Our so-called church music gets us into our feelings; we don't realize that we are getting into our flesh because feelings are *of* the flesh. Being sensual is not spiritual but of the flesh, and since there is no good thing in our flesh, we allow ourselves to be led by "no-good-thing." We listen to this sensual music when we need to know how to give reverence and respect. We do not know this because the music is nothing but "booty-shaking provocative rebellion."

We are always trying to shake our behinds, when we need to "go sit down somewhere" and *read* the Bible and *do* what it says. I enjoy this music, but I reject it as a form of worship. Why? Because who are we worshipping when we're doing the bump and grind to Jesus lyrics? Surely, this is strange fire and God commands us not to give him strange fire.[10]

LEADERSHIP LEADING TO WHAT?

We are messed up in every area. Getting degrees from Dumb-Roni Schools, but cannot master the subject matter. Getting Music Degrees and can't sight-read music. What kind of band director for a public school never picks up a score of music to teach a singing group? The kind who cannot read the music! What kind of PE teacher knows nothing about the sports game? What Science teacher doesn't know how to use a microscope? We get honorary church related degrees and don't differentiate between earned and honorary; we go to unaccredited schools and wonder why we can't get a job with these degrees; we buy degrees from degree mills and proudly display them on our walls and proudly although everybody knows it isn't worth the paper is it written on; and then we still fail to teach what we have learned from accredited schools. We are doing this to ourselves, not white folks. And these Dumb-Ronies are teaching our children in the public schools making our children as dumb as they are because, "You cannot teach what you do not know; and you can't lead where you don't go."

Check out the Job Descriptions requirements for Houston Independent School District (HISD), music teacher needing no musical ability, and Fort Bend Independent School District (FBISD), that only requires music teachers to play an instrument and not be tone death. They do not have to be able to sight-read

---

[10] And Nadab and Abihu died, when they offered strange fire before the LORD. (Number 26:61; KJV).

even though the State requirements dictate that music teachers are able to sight-read. **The State does not oversee or enforce the requirements even when they know the school districts are not cutting the mustard.** They need to make sure that Black children get these proficiencies the right-way or the academic way, instead of allowing incompetent Ronies to teach students to pick-up the music by teaching music incorrectly.

This is tragic because academically sound music instruction has far-reaching beneficial effects in increasing attention, improving test scores, building math and science skills, and peak performance for the brain that spills over to other subjects. Wrong-teaching results in disadvantage for black students. Wrong Teaching is worse than no teaching at all, because it is harder to correct wrong-teaching than to teach it correctly the first time.

Roni-teachers do not teach students by musical notation and the Solfege System of singing and playing music notes (the academic way). Instead, they teach students to listen to YouTube, to have church, to act inappropriately, leaving it up to the students to figure out the parts and music notation for themselves, never teaching people to play music through reading it from sheet music to sing properly or act properly—resulting in faulty learning. They are learning by "feeling" instead of learning by "thinking." This is not good because thinking is the only way to sharpen the mind for success. This NWord take-over in the school system causes us to provide an inferior education to our own children—Roni-making by Roni-teachers to our young—as we transmit being dumb to ourselves.

We get other degrees, but do not and cannot pass the qualifying state licensing tests. We can get our Head-Ronies-In-Charge to hire us when we know nothing, but we do this at the sacrifice of our children who are going to the schools with Dumb-Ronies-in-Charge, lowering the standard of excellence everywhere we go, and we transmit substandard learning causing a Roni-takeover of disrespect, mediocrity and ignorance in America. This is evidenced by the fact that, "We have an HNIC of the White House and he is a White man," who typifies this Roni-takeover of America. What leaders do, the populace follows and character and excellence have become nil. Consequently, our students cannot compete in mainstream educational systems and are left to the market of getting worthless credentials. This creates a world of non-standard educational systems that leaves Ronies to Ronies. Certainly, I don't want any goods or services from these substandard systems.

This is especially true for health care and public services workers who come to work looking for affirmation from the patients. I'd sure wouldn't leave my mother is these so called hospitals where staff react to patients and call it, "I'm human too." We are paid to take crap off patients who are sick, down, and hopeless, and if we can't understand that "The customer is always right," we need to go find another profession. If we are looking for validation, we need to find another profession, because patients do not have a code-of-ethics. They are not required to do anything a certain way and we are to meet them wherever they are. The Roni-mentality is taking over everywhere, in all aspects of society, and all (yellow, red, brown, black, and white) are acting this mentality out in unawareness that public servants and healthcare workers are excused to react to consumers. The thought of being dependent on these persons in a hospital, nursing home, daycare or school? On the clock, but not at work. Scary!

RONI'S LACK OF WORK ETHICS:

To *all* Managers of Ronies working in Public Services and HealthCare, you must understand that Ronies are provided healthcare and services primarily through Roni workers, so, "the rules are not real," and "they don't want to work," so, you must tell them they must be physically and psychologically present at work. When they are physically there, their hearts and minds are far from there. This causes them to be not psychologically present, and to be discourteous, unprofessional, uncaring, neglectful, abusive, and life threatening/deadly. Now remember Roni is a character not a color.

I pity the fooled (deceived naive victims) who end in the care of a bunch of Ronies in public services, personal care homes, hospitals, schools, or nursing homes, where services to the poor are overrun with Ronies-in-charge. These places are largely staffed with bad-acting Ronies of all kinds, especially African ones, bad-acting American Ronies, and bad-acting White-Ronies.

If you manage these folks, you must say to them:

1. YOU MAY ONLY TALK ABOUT WHAT IS NECESSARY TO DO THIS JOB WHILE ON THIS JOB:
You must tell them, "Don't talk about anything but this job while you are on the job," because they will talk all day about their business, their children, their clothes, their hair weaves/ hairdos/nails, their baby's daddy, boyfriends and husbands, and not do any work. If you do not tell them this, they will not be able to do the job for talking about their own concerns; they are not mentally present, are neglectful, and are abusive to patients/ customers.

2. YOU MUST BE ALL HERE WHEN YOU ARE WORKING HERE, NOT WITH YOUR MIND ON THINGS OUTSIDE OF THE JOB WHILE YOU ARE ON THE JOB:
Because they will just be going through the motions, but not doing what is necessary to be effective and curative on the job.

3. YOU MAY NOT TALK LIKE YOU ARE AT HOME (IN AN INFORMAL SETTING) WHEN ON THIS JOB:
Because if you do not tell them this, they will be too common, too colloquial, without proper boundaries, without good

understanding, and without any empathy while doing the job, thus exposing patients to neglect, unresponsiveness, indifference, and abuse.

4. YOU ARE TO BE COURTEOUS AND PROFESSIONAL AT ALL TIMES

Because if you don't tell them, they will respond right back to patients, consumers, or clients in the same manner clients respond to them, when they are *supposed* to treat consumers, patients, and clients with courtesy and professionalism no matter how the consumer, patient, or client treats them.

5. YOU MAY NOT PLACATE CUSTOMERS - YOU ARE TO INTERACT (connect, cooperate, and give closure) WITH THEM AND GIVE THEM SOLUTIONS:

If you don't, they will merely tell patients things like, "I'm sorry that happened to you," but will not do anything to help or resolve the problem. For example, telling patients to redirect other patients who are threatening, bothering, or violating them. Saying of a rude worker, "That's just the way he/she is," but not addressing the problem of the worker's bad attitude, wrong responses to patients, tardiness, inappropriate answers, angry responses, and counter-transference (reacting in the same manner sick and mentally impaired patients react to them). Roni workers live out their substandard subculture of bad-manners, unresponsiveness, indifference, neglect, and abuse in wide-open silence—everybody knows they *ain't doing nothing*, but do nothing about it. So you must make them do right.

6. YOU MUST PRACTICE INTEGRITY:

Personal integrity is evidenced by what a person does when no one is looking. You must build in an accountability system, because if you do not let them know they are being watched, they will treat people any-kind-of-way.

7. DO NOT SIT AROUND TALKING. ATTEND TO THE WRITTEN JOB DESCRIPTION:

If you don't say this to them, they will be on the clock but not on the job.

8. YOU MUST PERFORM TO THE ACADEMIC STANDARD TO WORK HERE:

You must let Roni know that he/she will not be able to do whatever he/she wants to do on the job, that there are standards that must be upheld and these are not MY standards but THE standards. When Roni doesn't want to do the job correctly, he/she makes it about the supervisor, saying things like, "It's his/her way or the highway," because they want to do whatever their way any kind of way. You must hold them to the standard and not allow them to make it about you, because if you let them make it about you, you will not know why your position is not working or why your business is failing. You must make Roni perform to standard or you'll need to put him/her out to keep them from messing up the place.

> RONI DOES NOT WANT TO WORK, AND DOES NOT BELIEVE THE RULES ARE REAL.

Remember, managers and supervisors, if you do not make Roni work, he/she is not going to do it, because Roni doesn't want to work. The rules are not real. They will neglect and abuse patients/customers/students, etc. if there is no one watching and if nobody is present to demonstrate caring for your loved ones.

RONI'S NEGLECT AND UNRESPONSIVENESS:

To family members (take special note if your loved ones are elderly or disabled), many public services and state and government agencies are staffed by Ronies (cheap labor market with wrong-learning degrees and certificates), so please know that Roni doesn't want to work for his/her pay, and wants to get something for free.

To Roni, the rules are not real. Roni will neglect, abuse, and kill your loved ones, and think *sorry* is a sufficient response to their negligence, especially if they don't think that anyone cares. Roni-staffed operations (schools, medical facilities, hospitals, nursing homes, and personal care homes) will not care unless you show them that *you* care.

Showing you care requires:

1. That you let Roni businesses know you will report them to Health and Protective Services Authorities, otherwise they will only straighten up while the policing agencies are on-site. Afterward, they will return to the same bad-acting and lazy folks they are when no one is looking.

The Health Department does not notify these operations of an inspection beforehand because Ronies pad records and straighten up temporarily if they are tipped off. The Health Department will sanction those who are not open and public with their complaints due to whistle blower's protection laws.

Roni-businesses must know that you are watching and will hold them accountable at all times, or they will just go through the motions, doing nothing or the least possible to look busy.

2. That you document problems encountered and do not trust anything they say—they will tell all kinds of lies to cover-up their negligence. Remember, not written, not done. For example, document in the following manner: (CHART NEXT PAGE)

Day/Date/ Time	Contact Person	Mode of Communication 1) Telcon to Phone# 2) On-site Conference	Problem/ Question	Staff Response	Unresolved Concern
1. Monday 7-12-15 1:30pm	Mary Doe, Nursing Supervisor	#2- OCS	Has not had a bath in a week	I don't know why?	What is the solution? Problem still unresolved.
2. Any day/date/ time	John Doe, Mgr	#1-Telcon (111) 111-1111	Patient is being hit by roommate	Not my job; I will refer to someone else	Patient in danger- unresolved

3. That you must *demonstrate* caring for your loved ones because the rules are not real with Roni; she/he tells you one thing and does another, or says she/he does one thing and does another. Roni is all about talk and does not walk the walk or his own talk.

Roni thinks "I don't know," by itself, is okay. This is unacceptable. *I don't knows* are always to be followed with, *But I'll find out.*

Taking these steps is the only way you can be reasonably sure that Roni workers will be psychologically present, courteous, professional, caring, attentive, and not neglectful, unresponsive, and abusive. That they will be healing and not life threatening—or even deadly—to your loved one. All lives do matter, but through a walk, not just talk!

So to the question, why a Roni Test? The test will help us measure where we are so we can determine where we need to improve. We must first recognize the problem before we can rectify it. Godspeed with this!

CHAPTER 4   EXCUSES, EXCUSES, EXCUSES

I'm Sick and Tired of Ronies, TOO!
Though many think it only applies to sisters and brothers,
Big Mama told me, "You know Ronies come in all colors!"

In every race they are the annoying ones everybody hates,
God forbid them to become your neighbor or ask for a date,

They disgust our temperaments with their intrusive speech,
They baffle our minds with their attitudes out of reach,

They cloud our eyesight with a hideously messy place,
They play their music to annoy our ears in our own space,

They test our best Christian ethic to unconditionally love,
They make us ashamed to be a member of the same club,

I'm 'specially sick and tired of the "Ronies" who look black like
me, Shallow minds not knowing the difference cannot see,

I can't fault White America for fearing the things we do,
My God, I'm scared when I see us grouped up too!

Whites have their own share of White Ronies to fight,
They call them po-white-trash, but they're harder to sight,

Too bad for *us* appearance is such a distinguishing factor,
Discriminating between friends and foes becomes a disaster!

Then there are Ronies of another kind called peckerwoods,
KKK offspring who flee minorities to secluded neighborhoods,

In their hearts they are murders that hate without a cause,
As if they're better when we're all the same otherwise after all,

Then there are other breeds of Ronies of a foreign race,
Trashing nice neighborhoods with group homes and auto
mechanics trade,

Filling it with trailers, junk and garages filled with clutter,
They create a groaning in our hearts that cannot be uttered,

I'm sick and tired of Ronies of all races, creeds, and colors,
I wish all mankind would respect all others as brothers,

All society cries out, "We're sick and tired of Ronies, too!"
'Cause, all humanity has to suffer the vexing things they do.

Justifying and Blaming our Wrongs

When Roni takes over and misses the mark, Roni makes excuses. Missing the mark, and in justifying missing-the-mark, saying, "I teach my way," when it's the wrong way. And these same incompetent teachers come to the school, church, and job the wrong way, as well. We are sub-standard everywhere we go.

The Roni-takeover among Blacks has less to do with White folks, although White-folks make the polices that inflict substandard teaching through *institutional racism*[11], but Black people accept this and accommodate substandard expectations. For the most part it is Ronies hiring and covering up other dumb Ronies with worthless degrees who also miss the mark.

There are societal standards that stack the odds against us. However, blaming others for our situation is a Roni practice. As a Black culture, we must not blame. We must assume responsibility for our own place in life. We just shake and fake everything because we would rather get one over on everybody instead of doing the job right. Dumb-Roni preachers miss the mark, so they put other dumb-Ronies in charge of Ronies who also miss the mark. Ronies who miss the mark also get jobs in the educational system, but the system employs these substandard Roni-teachers in the Roni-schools knowing they miss the mark. This causes students to be unable to compete in the real world, which robs them of opportunities for success.

> THERE ARE SOCIETAL STANDARDS THAT STACK THE ODDS AGAINST US AND BLAMING OTHERS FOR OUR SITUATION IS A RONI PRACTICE. AS A BLACK CULTURE, WE MUST ASSUME RESPONSIBILITY FOR OUR OWN PLACE IN LIFE.

EXCUSES FOR INCOMPETENCE/FAILURE

We've taken music completely out of the learning mode and made it all about what we feel, so learning music *by the book* is not an option anymore. We have Ronies who have degrees, but they have no knowledge, so they can't teach us what they don't know. Roni-musicians who strive to keep the music of the church academic, sacred, and reverent are rare. Ronies only want to

---

[11] The prediction of decisions on policies on the basis of racial inequality that disadvantages black people.

jump and scream in church, calling it *the Spirit,* when it is only a response to a feeling. These *feelings* are cultural and learned, and have nothing to do with the Spirit of God, rather the spirit of the devil, being lust, rebellion, and mind-control.

The main excuses we use to justify our wrong behavior are:

1. IT HAPPENED TO ME.
This doesn't fly because if it happened to you and you didn't like it, why would you do it to someone else or not stop what you didn't like?

2. WE ARE OPPRESSED.
This doesn't fly because treating other people like we want to be treated is all we need to do the right thing by others. We use the "oppressed" card anytime we want to justify our wrong behavior, but the question is, "What is the oppressed doing oppressing others?" It doesn't make sense.

3. I'M POOR AND HAVE NO CHOICE IN WHAT TO DO.
This doesn't fly because although crime is correlated to poverty, crime is not justified by poverty, and poverty is not the cause of crime. People in poverty must understand that America is the seat of opportunity. But when opportunity does not meet with preparation, then there will be no success. We must stop making excuses and admit the truth: we don't want to show up in our own lives, so we get tricked. And we are tricked by our own lies! To this, Big Mama said, "All excuses are lies!"

4. I AM INNOCENT (WHEN REALLY I AM GUILTY).
Saying, "They just don't like me," to deflect your own blameworthiness.

5. I LEARNED WRONGLY, HAVE MENTAL PROBLEMS, cannot do any better, don't know any better, am disadvantaged, was abused by my parents, didn't take my medicine today, etc.,

doesn't fly because society requires "some act-right" no matter what our problems/situations are; and anyone who fails to act-right will be left behind/excluded. Thus those in charge must insist, "You've got to get some act-right to make it in this world," with zero tolerance for any excuses for any reason. My Big Mama told me this way, "I don't care if you are blind, crippled, dumb, stupid, lazy, or crazy, you'd better act right until you get right or I'm gonna put something on your behind;" and I got it together. I'm glad I had no other option other than to act-right; I know this is a different day, but we must figure out ways to give our children no other way out other than to act-right, so that we will not be setting them up for failure, and then blaming it on the white man, when we are the only ones interacting with them.

6. THE SYSTEM SET ME UP TO FAIL (because my father was absent, because I am black, because I am poor, because I don't have an education, etc.): This does not fly because just because a trap is there doesn't mean you have to step into it. You're not a freaking mouse desperate for cheese in a mousetrap! You can hear, think, and see; so why are you getting caught in a trap?

The why's must only be used to determine the "how's" to fix the problem, but never as excuses or justification for not acting-right!

Because... *the grace of God that brings salvation has appeared to all men (everyone). It teaches us to say "No" to ungodliness and worldly passions, and to live self-controlled, upright and godly lives in this present age* (Titus 2:11-12; NIV).

TV EVANGELISTS AND MIND CONTROL

Mind control by TV Evangelist and Preachers in the False-Church deceive us as well, but we love being tricked. *Pitiful ain't it?* White and Black charlatan preachers tricking dumb-Ronies!

Dumb-Ronies follow TV evangelists more than any other group because we want an idol. Also we get tricked by Roni-preachers, who are black and white men, because we are lazy and don't want to work; even as a part of faith that clearly states, "faith without works is dead (James 2:20)." We would rather try to pay for the blessings of God and believe in a false hope. We are tricked by TV preachers and give them millions of dollars, while these fakes are lying about being healed.

You cannot buy a blessing. We need to stop this. It is senseless that we cannot pay our rent and bills, but are giving our money to fake TV preachers. I wish those TV evangelists would "Pop off" with medical verifications of their healings, when these fake healings have been reported for years and years.[12] But do we care? No! We'd rather be lied to and tricked than to believe God and work for what we want. I see why my Dad said, "I hate dumb N—."

OUR EXCUSES FOR NOT THINKING FOR OURSELVES

Ronies need to stop this foolishness of following these kinds of false preachers and false prophets, while also discrediting God to unbelievers. Church-Ronies are the craziest people in the world. We are the ones mostly following false prophets, because we'd rather believe lies than the truth. We want something for nothing, and don't want to work for what we want, not even to produce faith in God, also wanting God to give us something for free. The Roni-mentality is among us even in our pseudo-spirituality because we always want something for nothing. We want to get one over even on God. Roni doesn't want to put in the work to get what he/she wants and hates on those of us who do put in the work to succeed.

We are always being tricked by other folks, and being tricked by ourselves, and by White TV evangelists, Roni-pastors and

---

[12] "Peter Popoff," retrieved May 15, 2016 from: https://en.wikipedia.org/wiki/Peter_Popoff

preachers, fake-friends, lousy-lovers, and phony-family.

What took our Mega Church Leaders so long to speak up about togetherness, respect, and kindness, when all of our black sons were being killed by policeman? The lives of our Black Sons deserved some speaking up as well!

UNACCOUNTABLE FAKE FRIENDS

Sadly, real friendship is hard, if not impossible, among Ronies. Especially with church-Ronies, because many church folks among blacks are Ronies.

I was talking to a friend who is a true friend—someone who has all of three qualities of a trustworthy person: good boundaries, empathy, and understanding.[13] He cares for me and always lets me know what is on his mind regarding me. I talked to him about me getting a life insurance license and my rep's request to refer some nice people who wanted to improve their lives and build an estate.

> WE DISCRIMINATE AGAINST ONE ANOTHER MORE ABOUT HAIR TEXTURE AND SKIN COLOR THAN WHITE FOLKS DO.

"I don't really know a lot of nice Black people, especially people who want to change for the better," I said. He responded, "It's not that there are not nice Black people; it's the church-Ronies who don't want to improve and learn. So if you go to church, you won't know very many nice people."[14]

What's our excuse for being messy? For all of the teasing, taunting, low-rating, and bullying? *Us's is really against us's when it comes to teasing, taunting, and bullying each other.*

We lie and say we mean no harm because we do not have

---

[13] Hirsch, Victor, PhD, Contents of Therapy Question, "Make a list of the people you know who have, all three qualities, i.e., good boundaries, empathy, and understanding? These are the people who are trustworthy to have in your inner circle." Psychotherapy Session, March 31, 2015.
[14] Telcon with D. Staggers, December, 2015.

good manners, and we do not have good boundaries, empathy, or understanding. If we tried to count the people we know with these three qualities, we couldn't come up with enough to fill both our hands. This is because we are so disrespectful to one another, play with people about serious matters, and talk badly about those who cannot help the way they look (their hair texture, and their body size). The work we put into this mess is unbelievable. Why us, God? Yes, we have many obstacles in this world, but *we's racist against our own selves, too,* discriminating against those with physical features that are most unlike the physical features of white America.

SELF-LOATHING?

Rejection and low self-esteem is high among us because of the mean, low-down, and nasty ways we treat each other. Aside from being mean with our teasing, we get too common with each other and disregard proper boundaries, talking about private matters in public, laughing at people falling, making uncaring statements about another's downfall, looks, body weight, and general discourtesy. Who does that? Who low-rates people about their appearance, their illnesses, their size, their color, and their hair? Nobody but, Ronies-Of-All-Colors!

I do understand how rejection from those who are to affirm us can affect us because I was rejected early in life. This rejection was accompanied by mommy and daddy issues, bad-blood, i.e., I had some faulty learning from my upbringing and detrimental characteristics handed down from my bloodline, which included my ancestry in the shame of Ham who looked upon his father's nakedness.

We really need Jesus because we have the curse of rejection from America's slavery, racism, and the curse of the predispositions of our forefathers, upbringing, and bad-blood—these things which are non-existent to those who love God.

STOP LIVING OUT THE CURSE

We do nothing to help ourselves or demonstrate that we are not rejected, despised, and cursed with the way we treat each other and the way we "look" to the world. We have choice even with the curse of rejection and bad blood, but we must choose Jesus Christ—The King—to be made righteous, and we will not be subject to the curses, rejection, or bad blood that zeroed us out in the first place, i.e., what made us nothing to ourselves.

I was zeroed out by being rejection before and after I was born, but just because I felt like a zero, I didn't act like a zero. No excuses were acceptable for me and I had only one option—to act right—so I faked it until I made it, or acted right until I got right. Like so, we must act right until we get right and stop blaming the devil, God, white folks, slavery and life circumstances, because you will stand before God and the excuses won't be accepted; so why think the excuses matter now? We need Jesus and we need to help each other, not put each other down. It is very hard to get well among Roni because whatever pain you have from past rejection, hurt, and bad-blood, they make it worse by low-rating you, teasing you, and pouring salt in your wounds. You must get over it; get over what people think and what they say because Roni is heartless and knows he can hurt you.

> WE NEED TO PULL EACH OTHER UP AND OUT, AND NOT YANK ONE ANOTHER BACK TO THE BOTTOM OF THE BOWL.

We need Jesus and we need to help each other, not put each other down. It is very hard to get well among Roni because whatever pain you have from past rejection, hurt, and bad-blood, they make it worse by low-rating you, teasing you, and pouring salt in your wounds. You must *get over it;* get over what people think and what they say because Roni is heartless and knows he can hurt you.

I overcame Roni despite his abuse because I did not give Roni's words or thoughts any power. Why should I listen to Roni when Roni is nobody to me? Just as we chose to put someone down, we can chose to lift them up. We would see ourselves emerge out of the crawfish bowl altogether if we would only pull each other up and out, and not yank one another back down to the bottom of the bowl.

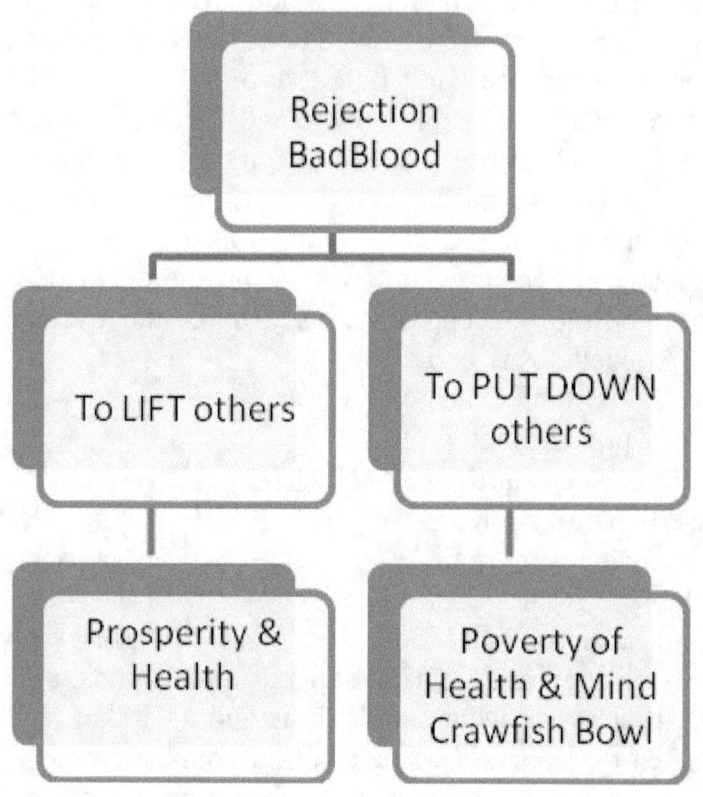

I could have very well taken the downward road because I always felt "less than," "worthless," "undeserving," as a result of the curses of rejection and bad-blood. But I rejected the curses and accepted the one who overcame all curses—Christ. *Christ redeemed us from the curse of the law, being made a curse for*

us: for it is written, Cursed is every one that hangeth on a tree (Gal. 3:13; KJV). Life is hard when we have to come against rejection and bad-blood, but we still have the *choice* to overcome these enemies. We need to stop putting each other down; when we lift others, we lift ourselves. It is tragic to see how we put ourselves down by the way we put each other down.

SYSTEM- AND SELF-PERPETUATED INFERIORITY COMPLEXES

We have to fight against the system-perpetuated and self-perpetuated inferiority complexes. The system predicts decisions and policies that negatively affect us exclusively as a racial group, resulting in racism and self-inflictors that create an environment that robs us of the ability to know anything of value. Both make us unable to think, and since we cannot think, we cannot hear the voice of the King. It is a bed of thorns to live among Roni with this double-edged hatchet—racism and Roni. Ronies have chopped us up long before the racist can get to us. The result being, the racists don't have to do the job because Roni is doing it for them.

> RACISTS DO NOT HAVE TO DESTROY US, BECAUSE RONI IS DOING IT FOR THEM.

Worst of all, the system-perpetuated complex is a major social system—public education—that subjects minorities to wrong teaching from Roni-teachers that limits our children's resources for success due to inferior training by inferior instructors which serves the system's institutional racism. This system allows dumb-Ronies with degrees to have charge of our children, and these teachers do not have the basic skills to teach. Like music teachers who cannot read music, speech teachers who cannot articulate words, social science teachers who cannot teach social research, and teachers who will not and cannot do the job because they will not follow the teacher's manual. This is how we make gray what we cannot see—institutional racism (when the whole system including Blacks and Whites are doing it) more than individual racism (when only one person is doing it).

Institutional Racism is the result of the Roni-making by Ronies in charge together with Roni-taking and breaking by White folks (also called The System and Larger Society). Although we fuss about individual and institutional racism, we are as part of the process—*because we gets our folks ready to be discriminated against* through Wrongful Collateral Damage by making them Ronies. When incompetent Roni-teachers give wrong-teaching to our children, it helps White folks keep us down with their Institutional Racism.

The incompetent Roni-teachers say, "I don't do things like everybody else. I do it my way!" They say this to justify their incompetence and wrong teaching, when academic instruction should be constant and standard for every competent educator. Education has been

> THE RIGHT-WAY IS ONE WAY AND ANY OTHER WAY (YOUR WAY) IS THE WRONG-WAY.

around for thousands of years. Since when did anyone make his or her own way, other than the right way? Still, incompetent Roni-teachers and dumb-Ronies say these things and we just accept it. They are telling us that they are teaching a substandard pedagogy to our children and we accept it. Who does that?

The White folks just takes advantage of the Ronies we done made and that's how we get Institutional Racism that can't hardly be seen, 'cause it operates through mixing us together. But we's all responsible for this evil. You see, Blacks against Blacks is so bad until you can't trust the so-called professionals of our kind. They will throw us under a bus, especially Roni-lawyers, businessmen and business women.

If it's Black and you don't know it's an Oreo cookie, don't touch it because you might be getting a Roni, and nobody has time for getting messed over by Roni lawyers, doctors, salesmen, school teachers, and so-called Roni professionals. We don't stand a chance anywhere we go: at home, at school, in business, in the community, or at church. Especially when we live in the gray of unawareness, Ronies throwing us under the bus when we do business with them. How can we expect White folks to give us a fair chance when we don't even give ourselves one? If we walk in *the light* we will not be fooled by *the gray*, but we cannot walk in the light because nobody teaches us that rules are real. But Roni, **Rules Are Real!**

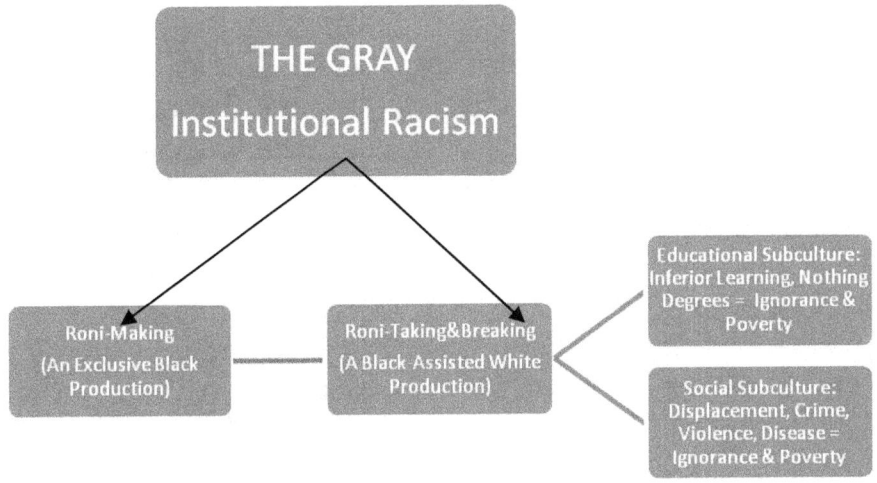

Sadly, institutional racism is real. It is the prediction of decisions and policies that debase people based on racial disparities/stereotypes. And this is hard to fight. But any foe is best fought when we are in the seat of "rightness." The working together of us making ourselves inferior through the lack of knowledge along with what the larger society's view of and treatment of us as inferior (profiling) accounts for a subculture fully functioning in unawareness of the disparity it is both party to and a victim of. Both educational disadvantage and socio-economic disadvantage plays into this lack of awareness. Problem is anything that cannot be measured does not exist and anything that cannot be measured cannot be remedied. So we must first stop making excuses; then we can hold the system accountable.

THE DETHRONEMENT OF GOD

Sadly, the Roni-church makes Roni big for a selfish benefit and dethrones God to do it, by putting our leaders in God's seat. They teach us to have magical thinking distracting us from hearing the Voice and then they put themselves in God's seat making themselves the voice that we should hear when they should teach us to hear the Voice of God. When they get hold of our minds, they teach us that we do not have any goodness in us. That we are helpless in doing right because the Spirit is going to do everything for us. They teach us that we are helpless over everything—God's wrath and Satan's evil. They don't teach us that God is in all of us, that we have some good in us, and that we are to do what we know is good and depend on God to do what we cannot do. We teach ourselves the wrong way so the ones in charge can be more than the ones below. But we are keeping all of us down by teaching us that God is going to do everything and *we ain't got to do nothing,* because Jesus did everything for us on that old rugged cross. Who believes that and who does that? Only dumb Ronies who do not want to do right or work for anything, not even their salvation.

Luke 9:23: And he said to them all, If any man will come after me, let him deny himself, and take up his cross daily, and follow me.

Fooled: I Thought I Tricked My Daddy
Into Eating Half Of The Earthworm!

Daddy, I've found an earthworm and I want to eat it!
Son, No! You can't eat an earthworm;
Please Daddy, I want to eat the earthworm!
Now Son, You don't need to eat the earthworm;
Daddy I'm begging you; Boo Hoo!
Can I please eat the earthworm?
Okay Son; go ahead if you want to eat it; go ahead and eat it!
But Daddy, I want you to eat half of the earthworm!
No, Son! I'm not going to eat half of the earthworm!
Daddy, Daddy, please I want you to eat half of it!
No! I'm not eating half of the earthworm!
Daddy, Daddy, Would you please eat half of it?
No Son! I'm not eating half of the earthworm;
do you understand?
Daddy, Daddy, Boo Hoo!
Please eat half of the earthworm… for me?
If you eat it, I'll be a good boy and do everything you say.
Okay, okay, Son, I'll eat half of the earthworm, for you.
But Daddy, I want you to go first!
Son, it's your earthworm. You go first.
Daddy! Daddy! Please go first? Please go first? Please, Daddy?
Okay, okay, Son, I'll eat my half first;
Thank you sooooooo much, Daddy!
(Daddy eats half first)
Boo…hoo…boo…hoo…!
What's wrong now, Son?
You…ate…my…half…Daddy!
How are your excuses working for you?

My Daddy, Abba, God came from Heaven
to eat my half of the earthworm,

But immediately after he'd eaten his half, I began to squirm,
I changed my mind about eating my half
blaming him for eating my part,
Yet, I was the one he'd eaten it for
because I was the one left in the dark,
Jesus' work on Calvary is a finished work
of The Cross already done,
But this is Jesus' part and we must do our part
so our race will be won,
God is working on us, but we're supposed to be
working on ourselves too,
For Him to eat His half and me not eat my half
was a tacky thing to do,
I knew what I did, but convinced myself
I should let Him eat it alone,
I fooled myself into thinking this wouldn't
keep me from getting home,
Many times I asked, "Should I eat my half or take
His sharing in vain?
After He'd eaten His part, I owned His pleasure,
but I disowned His pain!
Must Jesus Christ bear the cross all alone
and the entire world go free?
No! There is a cross for every one of us
and there is a cross for me!

THE DEMORALIZATION OF PEOPLE WITH N— THEOLOGY

Theological excuses! The Roni-church helps the State make financial gains from exploitation of church Ronies by demoralizing us and giving us over to the jail, hell on earth, and hell in eternity, since they teach us to violate the First Commandment. The church and the State tell everyone that they are separated when they are actually married. This lie is their strategy to benefit from the disadvantages the church and the State have created for Roni.

The All Factor—we know that *all* clergy *do not* make Roni fatter, but the problem is that there are so many who *do* that it appears to be all. There are many upstanding clergypersons who are trying to make Roni skinny, but not enough, and these leaders are discredited by Roni to keep the focus off what they are doing wrong by making *it* about someone else. So they holler, "You think you are better than me?" meaning *they think you are better than them*, when nobody is any better. However, some are better off because they work, go to school, and follow rules. They say, "Don't judge," meaning *don't evaluate what you see me doing.* They holler, "Be patient," meaning *lower the standard and let me do it any kind of way*. Ronies make three main arguments against any kind of *act-right,* mostly when Roni-makers wrap a false theology around the practices of people doing whatever they want to do, people lowering the minimum standard for achieving a task or earning an educational proficiency and people who do not want to do what is right. We are so good at what we do until we don't know that we can't merely stir up what's in us; we need to study, too. But many of us don't want to stir or study when we need to stir and study.

A lopsided group of Roni-leaders learned that they could benefit from my advantage without me benefiting, and I participated in this. It was a double convenience—I felt justified in my wrongdoing and they were not accountable for their wrongdoing. This particular group of Roni-preachers knew that I was extremely religious and super spiritual. They knew I had an insatiable desire for God, so they used their preaching to focus on people instead of God—they tried to use God. They pointed me toward themselves and not to the King. They knew I did not and would not read, so they made sure I stayed in the dark about who I was supposed to be—child of the King, not a child of darkness; a follower of Christ, not a follower of men; a Daughter of Zion, not in a harem for men. In their harems, they kept secrets with all of the women, never choosing one because they could not afford to pick one of the hens in the henhouse. They wanted all of them and could have them all. They do not have to get married because they can have all the women, and benefit financially from their foolishness, allowing these pimp-daddy gangster Roni-preachers to use them.

Racists may be confused because there is a lopsided number of those who look like Roni represented in the church, represented in jails/prison, involved in violence, who have sexually transmitted diseases, and live in poverty, until it looks like all of that color are the same. One thing is for sure, the hardest thing about being Black is not what Whites are doing; the hardest thing about being Black is living among broke Ronies who are always trying to get something for nothing and hit you up for money; speak evil of you because you won't be a part of their begging program; and they hate you when you have your own stuff. Roni is a threat to everybody, even to those who resemble Roni.

Concluding our discussion about excuses, we must stop the excuses because they are lies and do not justify poor conduct and poor pockets. Yes, we have obstacles, but an excuse is one thing and an obstacle is another. Obstacles can be overcome, but excuses have no resolution.

Stop making excuses and start making progress.

Godspeed with this!

CHAPTER 5   DUAL REALIZATION

White Supremacy and Racism + Roni Mess = A Black Person's Nightmare. Sadly, a Black person has nowhere to fit in America. White folks see us as "know it all niggers," and black-Ronies see us as, "want-to-be-white folk-niggers." We get it from both sides, but are still treated as niggers no matter what we accomplish. Either way, living among Whites or Blacks is hard for persons of color caught between Racism and Ronism. A black citizen is caught in the middle with no place to go. Outside hate from whites and inside self-hate from blacks makes the black existence most miserable. "Ronies are hell, give you hell, and will send you to hell," and there is no remedy of law for ronism; at least with racism the law does offer some remedy.

Roni is one thing and Black is another; don't get them twisted!

THE 80-90 THEORY

Living among Ronies, I experienced that eighty percent of those who look like me are Ronies and ninety percent of those Ronies are Church-Ronies. Thus, we live in a dual-reality. Failure to understand this dual-realization (or dualism) will cause a Black person to be completely unstable, because we must know how to handle this duality—racism and Roni. On one hand, there is racism, and on the other hand, there is the subculture of Roni that is equally difficult to live in. With the Racism-Roni Dualism that we experience, many of us have no place to fit in, because racists treat us like we are a Roni, and Roni demands that we act like Roni because Roni is all Roni understands.

Whites call intelligent black people, "know-it-all-Ronies," and Black Ronies call us, "Uppity Ronies." We are penalized all the more when we are not a dumb Roni. It is a lonely and hard existence to be born Black in America, because Roni is so big among us until people don't know the difference between Ronies and Black Americans. Then, the Roni-subculture demonstrates and fulfills racial stereotypes of Black people in a way that gives the appearance of all, causing all people of African descent to suffer the backlash of being perceived as Roni. But Black is one thing and Roni is another, and I must help society to realize the difference.

We have little to no help in changing this malignant perception of Roni as *all* Black people. For instance, poor grammar is considered a Black dialect, when *Ebonics* has nothing to do with our race but it has everything to do with poor grammar. We should not let society define us in this way. *The subculture is sustained by us* when we accept these kinds of paring with race and poor grammar. Ebonics may be spoken by a large percentage of Ronies who are Black, but this doesn't mean that Ebonics is Black. Ebonics is not a Black thing, but a language thing—bad English, not Black enunciation. Unfortunately, we have Roni preachers, Roni TV, radio, media, and Roni politicians making the subculture more visible, while misrepresenting Blacks who are a part of the mainstream culture. This is deception, but all Blacks suffer for it because this has misconstrued Blacks as niggers in everyone's minds, even in the minds of black people, seemingly in unawareness.

> EBONICS IS NOT A BLACK THING, BUT A LANGUAGE THING—BAD ENGLISH, NOT BLACK ENUNCIATION.

We Have Rules of Etiquette, Too

By the way, good manners, good citizenship, and Christianity are not "trying to be White," as Ronies say in an effort to keep us from being accountable for our actions. And there is nothing worse than Bible-slinging Ronies, confessing Jesus and conducting themselves like Satan, especially when the Roni is someone in leadership. Here is an example of Bible-slinging Ronies' faulty reasoning: *Do not trust us and do not put any confidence in what we say, because we have no regard for what is right and what is appropriate from the pulpit to the door. We are God's children who deserve to be loved and taught by instruction and example, but we don't want to learn anything that is correct and excellent.*

Talk It But Won't Walk It

A great deal of teaching by example is lost for those who are leaders in the black community. Roni-preachers who make it big have no regard for the Bible, even for the parts of the Bible they themselves preach and teach. They'll do anything, say anything, treat people any-kind-of way, have no integrity, and put themselves above the laws of God and the laws of the land. They have children outside of their marriages with women in their own churches, sexually assault children and their church members, have affairs with women in their churches knowingly to their wives, sons, and daughters, molest their own children, molest those they have power over, do all kinds of crooked money schemes, and participate in "drive-by" desecrations of the body, soul, and spirit of their followers right in front of Ronies who do and say nothing.

If you want to know what's wrong with the Black race look at the Black church and White preachers who exploit and trick Black people through religion. Ronies are sowing into bad ground and wondering why they never reap a harvest. This is a hell-bound cult with idolatry and worship of men who make slaves out of followers. We know it is not everyone, but it appears that a majority of these leaders fit the description, resulting in a lopsided appearance of all. There is an entire subculture of people running to conferences, looking for prophetic utterances which are nothing but sorcery, going to prayer conferences as if the heart does not know how to pray to God. This is big business for the so-called healers, prophets, conferences leaders, and prophetesses. And they don't even treat us with respect, yet we go and give our hard earned money looking for pies in the sky.

Consequently, the so-called Black church is famous for PRWN—Public Replacement Without Notice—using you until they see someone/something they think is better without having the decency to call the person ahead of time to let them know that they are no longer wanted. They also lie about unsuspecting persons to the police, wanting to shame and belittle them before jealous and hateful church members who joined the witch-hunt without even knowing why. As I see them, they are just low-down and dirty and will hurt you just as much as Caesar will and without any benefits or the protection of the law. Church leadership does this most with musicians, choir directors, and singers who have learned to prostitute themselves with these Roni-preachers. These worker bees aren't anything but commodities to the highest bidder, suiting the lusts and whims of people who worship men, money, and music. They will PRWN you and then PRWN the person they replaced you with. Making kings of themselves off the people's meager means. Roni-preachers use people and throw them away like Amnon did with Tamar after he violated her (2 Samuel 13:15). They will hate you worse than they did before they used you, and leave you with a broken heart that nobody lifts a finger to soothe.

These so-called leaders use God and Jesus' name to get what they want and they neither know Him nor worship Him.

Everything they do is so sensual and sexual including what they call worship, music, and preaching, while the church sits by and does nothing. This behavior excites their fleshly wrongdoing, leading them to all kinds of wrongdoing. Roni-preachers seduce the people into serving them in God's name and their allegiance is purely a soul-tie to the Roni-preacher, not to God. Most of our preachers are pimps in the push-pit not the pulpit, because they don't pull us up, they only push us down. They are the ones who prostitute, play, and seduce us with their sensuality and sex appeal, pointing us to Roni-dom instead of the Kingdom.

They disgrace us, and themselves, on reality TV and do not even know they are shaming all of us and the King. What they are doing has nothing to do with the Spirit. It is only about their charisma, popularity, fat pockets, and mind-control. Therefore, we learn to worship ourselves, to worship our *hungry-dogs-at-a-meat-house* leaders, to worship our *jungle-bunny exuberance*, to pimp God and buy blessings, and to worship our lust-provoking and sensual music that has no elements of sacredness.

It is almost impossible to stay grounded in who you are in these settings with all of the gyrations going on. Fact is, you do not have to move to feel His presence; how we decide to move is a choice and is culturally derived. God is not moving our bodies around. Jungle-bunnies with low esteem will not reap spiritual growth because they are doing nothing but basking in their flesh and sending up praise that God does not receive. So who is receiving our strange fire? Satan takes this for himself because God is not in our N– mess. We wonder why the Roni-church is so vile and wretched. Do we know what is really going on? It is dangerous spiritually to go to any church, but especially a Roni-church.

FAKE CHURCH

I must admit that since Roni has been a part of me, I love the frenzies, too; I just know it's not spiritual, but cathartic and stress-releasing. Roni thinks it's more spiritual and that it's going to change his life, when it is not going to change anything but the way he feels for a moment. Thus, Roni does nothing and expects God to make things happen. *And we don't even know we've been spit-out 'cause God ain't in our mess.* You can only believe a lie for so long, until you are deceived because the first lie tricks the one who tells it—me and you!

Looking for love in the Roni-church is looking for love in the wrong place because Ronies-In-Charge will take your cry for help as an opportunity to help themselves to your body, your money, and your mind. They will sexually assault you and preach from the pulpit as if they have done nothing wrong.

> CHURCH RONIES WORSHIP MUSIC, MONEY, MEN, AND FEELING GOOD.

Then when they get up to do their so-called preaching, not only do they make you feel bad about God, they also make you feel bad about yourself. Roni-preachers and so-called Bible teachers teach us that God, the church, and their voice is the same; so we don't know that God is one thing and the church is another, and we don't know that the preacher is only a messenger who is supposed to say it like God said it. We get these all twisted. Thus, we get tricked and used.

Yes, Ronies-In-Charge have a right to change their minds and hire who they want, but the problem is the way they do this with no integrity, no tact, and no consideration for the person they are hurting who has served faithfully. Ever heard of a Roni-preacher PRWNing a musician for protecting a female choir member from being sexually assaulted by the preacher's elderly lesbian sister? What should he have protected?

The Roni-church keeps children and working people up all night; the children can't get up and go to school on time and the adults can't go to work on time. This keeps us unprepared for a world that requires us to be educated and prepared to work gainfully. We are the poorest people on the earth because the pastors make their money off us and talk about what the Lord is going to do. All the while, we do nothing, making this the most detrimental part of the Roni-church; it makes us crazy, stupid-acting, and lazy.

Church Ronies worship music, money, men, and feeling good. They are always like junkies looking for another moment, so we never worship the King. This makes the Roni-church a terrible place to go for moral development. Until I was able to get out of the bottom of the bucket, I had to understand my dual existence, i.e., being with Roni, but not of Roni. And like I said, "The worst thing about being Black is Roni, not Whites."

> THE WORST THING ABOUT BEING BLACK IS BEING USED AND ABUSED BY BLACK-RONIES.

THE HARDEST THING ABOUT BEING BLACK

It is very difficult to live as a Black person because non-Ronies think that all of *my kind* is a Roni, and Ronies treat Black people like crap. We get it from both sides, tortured in Roniland as we have no place to voice our anguish about being tortured in Roni-dom. Everybody knows about White-racism, but nobody admits to suffering Black-Roni-mess, which is worse. Ronies will use, badger, and fight you (physically) about what you have earned until you end up as broke, busted, disgusted, and can't be trusted as they are.

I really had no place to go until I got out of the bottom of the bucket in Roni-dom and could only go up. The worst thing about being Black is more than being identified with and treated like Roni by Non-Ronies. The worst thing about being black is being used and abused by Black-Ronies; Roni does not want to work and would rather get one over on other people. They would rather beg than work, so when I see a beggar, I say, "I was in the same shape you're in. I just went to work, so I have nothing to give you."

Everyone who looks like us doesn't demonstrate being a Roni. Some have not been reared in a culture of Roni, but are middle-class citizens with a conscience aside from religion. Roni acts as if he has no good in him at all, and even with God, he has the *can't-help-its*. It is about character, not color, but when there are so many of color that do the wrong things, it appears it *is* about color and we are all the same.

Most Ronies do not know they are Ronies, or better said, do not know that they *act* like Ronies. I did not know I was Roni at first, because I was looking at everyone else and blaming everything outside of me for my problems. Something may

> IT IS ABOUT CHARACTER, NOT COLOR, BUT WHEN THERE ARE SO MANY OF COLOR THAT DO WRONG THINGS, IT APPEARS IT *IS* ABOUT COLOR AND WE ARE ALL THE SAME.

not be my fault, but it is still my problem. Just because I have a seemingly valid reason to do wrong doesn't mean I have an excuse to do wrong; the King nailed all our excuses to a cross. Big Mama said, "All excuses is lies." So I have to work and walk it out myself, whatever my road may be. Yes, it comes up, *"is my road fair"?* The answer is *no*. It is not fair, but it is real. I am the only one who can handle it. That is life.

THE TRUTH, NOT MY TRUTH

Fortunately, I have gotten enough education under my belt that I can step out of Roniland into a life of greater peace, but I care about Roni too much to leave them in the pit. Actually, I love Roni so much that I had to get the "beam" of self-will out of my eye as it was the Lord who anointed me as a seeker of truth. Consequently, I had to remove this beam of self-righteousness out of my own eye before I could attempt to remove the mote of bad-acting from Roni's eye. I learned to remain who I am, and not escalate, no matter what the situation. I learned I can be IN it and still not be OF it. I recognized that God gave me the will to do right, not me, and I asked Him to create in me the desire to do what is right (Psalms 51:9-11).

I do not want to be a hypocrite acting as if I am perfect, because I am

> I LEARNED RONI-DOM IS NOT THE WORLD; IT WAS ONLY MY WORLD AT THAT TIME.

certainly not. I only want to give my people the information we need to make an informed decision about how we demonstrate who we are. Being mindful of this is the only way I can be loving, long-suffering, and patient with those who have not overcome. My economic and social independence was all God's doing, not my own, and His voice inside me convinced me I could persevere even as the world around me was entirely negative and discouraging.

A WORLD BUT NOT THE WORLD

I've lived in the different world of Roni-dom and know that the worst thing I could have done was to believe what it taught me about myself—whatever Satan wanted me to believe. It was negative, hateful, cruelly jealous, envious, unlearned, ignorant, and discouraging, but it was not the world. It was only *my* world at *that* time. It was definitely *a* world, but it wasn't *the* world.

If you don't come to recognize that Roniland is not the world, you will be shaped into what the devil wants you to believe about yourself. I went into cultural shock when I entered Roniville, but I recovered because I rejected what Ronies had to say about me and learned to listen to God. The only thing Ronies know how to do it to put each other down. Ronies kill your self-esteem long before the White man oppresses you, and most of us never get into a position where we would generate any real racism, because we are only a threat to the social milieu, not to the economy.

I was in Roni-dom for a while, but I didn't stay until I forget who I am—someone who is leaning and depending on God to empower me to do what is right by God, myself and others. If we are not careful we can be sucked into Roni-dom—a place of prideful wrongdoing that refutes the consequences of our choices. Other biblical descriptions for this type of sinner are sluggard, slothful, heathen, fool, brawler, hell raiser, busybody, scorner, and erring one. Sadly, it's so hard to live among Roni who doesn't want to do right, doesn't want to pay for his wrongdoing, and gets mad at you when *you* do what's right and succeed. Covetousness and jealousy are intense demons we face in this dual existence, as well as ignorance and opportunism, with a total disregard for rules being first, never developing the kind of character that will give us credibility in the world.

At times, I am ashamed of being Black because Roni acts so badly in public. "My people, My people?" I can see why White-folks hate us, but just because we have a good reason to feel the way we do, doesn't mean we have a good reason to act the way we do, and this means any reason for bad acting—Target or Weapon.

Character transcends color, but when our bad character is bigger than our color, it looks like it is about our color rather than our character. We must work very hard until the transcending takes place, from seeing our color to seeing our character. I'm sure I had to work harder than Non-Blacks. We must understand that we live in a dual world, one of Ronies and one of non-Ronies and it will drive you crazy if you try to deny that Roni is real, so you have to know how to deal with Roni.

Yet, I don't deserve to be terrorized and killed; I deserve to be loved and taught by instruction and example. So regarding Dual Realism, we must learn to compartmentalize our relationships. We must also compartmentalize our environments. This means we divide our realities into categories, distinguishing between what is real and what is false. Roni-dom is a false reality of what living is about. It is a false picture of what success and the pursuit of happiness are as

> IT WILL DRIVE YOU CRAZY IF YOU TRY TO DENY THAT RONI IS REAL, SO YOU HAVE TO KNOW HOW TO DEAL WITH RONI.

it leads to poverty, disease, and destruction. When we understand this dualism, we can know how to respond in two worlds, IGNORANCE or ENLIGHTENMENT. We can live in enlightenment inside Roniville, because we have the power to be in the world but not of the world. Godspeed with this!

CHAPTER 6   THE PROBLEM IS BLINDNESS

THE BLIND LEADING THE BLIND

Lack of awareness, just like the Emperor in his new clothes[15], happens right in front of us, with everyone denying it. Thus, Roni-making takes place right in open view because we are blinded by our so-called Roni leaders; the blind lead the blind. We do not seem to know that we are not victims, but have made ourselves victims by our actions then we point the finger at someone else. We reproduce Ronies in the church house because church Ronies in-charge have taken over the role of non-Roni-slave masters. So Ronies are most often being led by these *hirelings* who call themselves shepherds, and the hirelings cast their blame on Satan, allowing them to operate in secrecy against Ronies.

Roni-preachers are wrongly pointing-out the wolf as the problem, calling the wolf the enemy when the only reason the wolf devoured us is because the Hireling-Church-Roni-In-Charge (HCRIC) let the wolf loose on us (the sheep). Church-Ronies in charge are there to fleece us, not feed us, and the flock is made to believe Satan is the target enemy. The hireling is our actual enemy, wolves-in-sheep's-clothes deceiving and devouring us. Our blind leaders lead blind followers and have brought the vast percentage of Ronies to a low place.

When I understood that I was a Roni because of what I had learned, I decided to unlearn what I knew, and learn what I needed to know. Unknowingly, I had been made into a bad-actor

---

[15] From: [http://andersen.sdu.dk/vaerk/hersholt/TheEmperorsNewClothes_e.html].

by bad-actors in charge in my world, but this learned behavior didn't work in the larger world. This Roni-world of substandard behavior is not acceptable outside and it makes the outside world hate us. We lower the standard inside, but the true standard remains the same outside, so we go into the world unprepared. We then play the race, grace, and helplessness card, but who is listening?

The world is moving on and we are left behind in stupidity and poverty. They are still locking us up and putting us out and we are forever learning but never coming into the knowledge of truth. No one should be put in this position unless they choose it with the eyes-open, not blindly. Therefore, I decided to step forward and speak out to help people to make a choice. Anyone can be a Roni, but you do not *have* to be one or act like one.

OPENING MY OWN EYES

I changed my actions. I started to think for myself. When I started to think for myself, I learned to look closely at myself. I had to unlearn learned helplessness and relearn faith. Then I had to put in the work to change for the better.

One thing for sure when you get ready to relearn, a teacher will show up. I understood how I was made into a Roni. So, I could relearn how to change my presentation. Nonetheless, there are some good things about knowing how and when to act like Roni, but it is good to know I have a choice. I don't necessarily have to act like a Roni, even if I was groomed into Roni. Although I did not choose my past, I can choose my future. The main thing I needed to be able to do is to be independent. I had to move my feet away from the mess I was in to a better place; to be in a good place instead of a bad place. I had to look to myself for answers that were right inside of me as everyone who was supposed to give me leadership was actually bringing me down. For instance, community activists...

BLINDED BY SO-CALLED CIVIL-RIGHTS LEADERS

Community activists taught me to feel victimized so that I thought I was helpless—that I couldn't do anything about my situation because it was society's fault, and since society didn't treat me the way I should be treated, I had an excuse to be nothing. Roni-so-called *activists* help us feel hopeless and helpless during Black history month. Instead of teaching us to celebrate our victories and current accomplishments, they teach us to rehearse our pain and self-inflicted suffering. Most of what we do ends up making us feel more helpless and

> INSTEAD OF TEACHING US TO CELEBRATE OUR VICTORIES AND CURRENT ACCOMPLISHMENTS, RONI ACTIVISTS TEACH US TO REHEARSE OUR PAIN AND SELF-INFLICTED SUFFERING.

sorry for ourselves, then we will not do anything about our bad-acting and laziness. This perpetuates our tendency to avoid academic education and gainful employment. We are taught helplessness by our own leaders.

BLINDED BY THE CHURCH

The church taught me to feel justified in wrongdoing, when it should have taught me to do the right thing without excuses. Instead, they teach me, 1.) *Nobody is perfect,* to justify me not being decent or improving my condition; 2.) *We are all sinners,* to give me an excuse to act ugly and not do the good that I know to do; 3.) *We should not judge,* to keep anyone from making us accountable for our actions; 4.) *You're not any better than me*, to use people as the measuring rod for behavior rather than accepting what God says is right and wrong.

The church taught me that I do not have to do what is right because God's grace covers up my wrongdoing, when grace is not covering anything up; it is giving us extended time to get it right. We never receive God's grace as a privilege because we're always trying to get by with wrongdoing. We have God all bent and twisted in the minds of people when He is nothing like what the church portrays. God is good and loves us all, but He does not reward wrong behavior and has prepared a place for those who have no regard for righteousness. Thus, the church teaches us a N— Theology rather than giving us the true message of Jesus Christ. We are to walk the way Christ walked, in obedience to the will of God, our Father, denying ourselves and practicing our faith as a discipline or regulation of wrongdoing.

BLINDED BY THE LAW

The law taught me that I am nothing, and I will be wrong even when I am right. It should have taught me that I have nothing to fear when I am right and that I will be vindicated when I am wronged. I understood the conspiracy between the state, the feds, the school, and the parents who are blindly participating in the demise of the young. They are participating in the in-education (not educating) of the Negro, which has now extended to all America's youth, more concerned with students passing their tests than actually learning the content.

On the contrary, when we know there will be justice when we do what is right, we must take our cases to the judge. The judge is accountable to the public for making just decisions. You must press on and bypass the riffraff and get it to the judge, then you'll be in a better position to see the system work for you. My story of how I got the system to work for me is recorded in my book, *Caesar Took My Cheese.*[16] The law will work for you, but you must go through the process. Don't go violent; go to Caesar with his decrees. Caesar must regard his own laws.

---

[16] *Caesar Took My Cheese: How to Keep Your Change in These Changing Times,* ISBN: 151186475, Vinedwellers Ministries Press, 2016

BLINDED BY TV

Television and radio taught me that I could be uncouth, uneducated, devious, criminal, and silly and still get rich. Roni-media poisons the minds of poor Ronies turning them against education and good manners, helping to keep them in poverty and prison. Roni TV teaches us to be emotionally needy, lowdown, licentious, messy, nosey, and discourteous, to tell our personal business, and to tend to everybody else's business instead of our own. We need to learn to tend to our own business and learn to get ahead the right way. We explain this as love, but if this is love who wants it? I surely do not want Roni's kind of love, which is nothing but control. The media take the worst of all actors and make them stars, making it look like that's the way Blacks act, when it's not about being Black; it's about being Roni. For example, Baltimore is not a Black thing; it's an N-Word thing. But news media has described it as a Black thing, thereby indicting all Black people to be unknowingly perceived as riotous and thieving. **That's not Black, that's Roni!**

> TELEVISION AND RADIO TAUGHT ME THAT I COULD BE UNCOUTH, UNEDUCATED, DEVIOUS, CRIMINAL, AND SILLY AND STILL GET RICH.

Ronies on the TV make the world think that being Roni is the same as being Black. By doing this, they promote the stereotypes that keep us enslaved in our minds and in our pockets. Equating Black with Roni is a great assault upon our image because this causes us to be lumped into the *lopsided appearance of all* and treated accordingly.

This book seeks to help resolve the evil that occurs through a joint effort with White-folks. We help them by mimicking Roni-TV stars, by jumping around to music when we're not in a dance hall, by shaking our butts all the time, by low-rating and bad-mouthing each other, by tearing up our neighborhoods and our own stuff, by failing to get a quality education, by supporting fly-by-night schools, by buying cheap clothes, by buying expensive tennis shoes, by wearing a $500 hat on a ten-cent head, by giving millions of dollars to TV evangelist and so-called prophets, and by showing ourselves to be common, disrespectful, and rude towards one another. The TV is the devil on us, just like we are.

Blind to Bad Boys vs. Good Man

Enabling mothers and absent fathers taught Roni-menfolk to be Mama's boys, not good men. They gave them a reason not to take care of their children, so the only thing that can make them act right is White policemen and White judges. They will not do what is right by their children unless they are forced and told to *do it the right-way or the White-way.* The right way is for them to tend to their responsibilities on their own, whereas, the White-way is to do it by force.

Under the White-way, they're going to do it; they're going to pay child support, but need to decide how they are going to do it—by force or by choice. Who does this? Who would accept disgrace over dignity? Roni does this, because this is what Ronies do. Ronies will not act right unless they are forced. I do not know why our mothers turn our men into pantywaists instead of making our sons strong and responsible men. They turn them into someone that no woman can live with or would want.

> RONIES WILL NOT ACT RIGHT UNLESS THEY ARE FORCED.

I do not know why absent fathers are always interfering and disappearing. They interfere with the right things the *here-and-now* parent is doing—sabotaging it, but disappear and fail to fix what they have messed up. I know they may get the short end of the stick a lot of times because the baby needs to stay with the mother if they break up, but if they would just be present in the heart of their children their love would be stronger than their absence from home. They become bitter instead of getting better, and they make life a living hell for themselves, their children, the mother, and everyone else involved.

At a conscious and unconscious level they believe all of Satan's lies taught to them by their enabling mothers, the church, society, the TV, and the politicians that give them cause to blame everything outside of themselves for their circumstances. They are completely out-of-control and under the submission of Satan doing his work on Earth. He kills what he is to protect. He hates what he is to love. He hurts what he is to help. He is the exact opposite of what God created him to be and does not know it. Especially when he goes to church, because he does not know that church is one thing and God is another. Just because you go to church does not mean the church is in you.

A church Roni-man will treat you worse than a street Roni-man. Big Mama used to say to us girls, "Scratch yo own itch and keep yo pride," and I added also, "to save yo hide," cause these low-down men will fool, forget you, and give you a deadly disease. So, "Scratch yo own itch to keep yo pride and save yo hide!" Leave these men alone until we can *unbrainwash* them. Sadly, they are "other directed" in their focus regarding their own lives, allowing them to have feelings of entitlement, feelings of helplessness, feelings of blaming, and feelings of ingratitude that render them irresponsible, unresponsive, and abusive to themselves and others. Our Roni-men are absent in their own lives, so how can you expect him to be present in your life? Even moving from place to place, seeking a failed relocation solution, when the problem is in their heads. Relocation will not change him because his problem is with him—in his Roni-head!

Women need to be independent in our pockets and in our minds. A woman must have her own money, because our men are too messed up to depend on. We need to be concerned with having our own money, not having our own man. The church doesn't help men to be responsible or faithful, but teaches them to be whores, sugar daddies, and players, saying to them, "men will be men," "it's a man's world," "a woman can't preach/teach men," and "a man is the head," without teaching him what "head" means (as Christ died for the church.)

CHECK YOURSELF, CHECK YOUR PREACHER

I didn't check myself, so I wrecked myself, because I acted badly—bad actor. I say *act* because sometimes our true self is not what we look or *act* like. We may not be aware of our own behavior and others can only go by what they see. *We* end up *acting out* against Sons and Daughters of the King—the kind of individuals we are supposed to be. We must make a conscious decision to strive for higher ground. We must make a conscious decision to be the individual God wants us to be. Unfortunately, I brought hurt into my life making life unnecessarily hard, unhappy, and unproductive for me and others. Sadly, anywhere there was a large concentration of me, there was destruction, violence, disease, and poverty. Everyone was scared when I moved into the neighborhood, even my look-a-likes. Since I do not know how to live among other people, neighborhoods created Home Owners Associations to keep me from tearing up the neighborhood. So the answer to, "What is an HOA?," is a group of property owners organized to keep Ronies from tearing up the neighborhood.

I went to church all of my life but didn't know it had anything to do with a divine being, namely, God. I never saw God in the church. I just thought people went there to take up money, show off their clothes, and buy the preacher and his family fancy cars and clothes. I could play music for them and I learned that I could control them with certain musical cadences. It was all a big game to me at first, until I had an experience with God many years down the road. I was devastated in the church anyway because the people were so mean and wicked. I became just as wicked and even more wicked to survive. **Black people are scared of Roni, too.**

I wished I'd known that God was real much sooner than I did because I could have been working for the Kingdom rather than building up Roni-dom like so many are doing now. This does not have to be the case. The more we do what is right, the more we will learn what is right. Doing what we know is right is a great start. Then doing the best we can with what we know is a great finish!

Blind to Not Demonstrating Who I Am

Most often we know what's right but refuse to do what we know and we have done wrong so long until we've made ourselves believe we are right. But, I need to remember not to kill, steal, or envy. I cannot worship any other person, place or thing, other than God, and I should treat other people the way I should be treated. The Six Lessons in this book are a good way to start on a new path toward true freedom. I must only worship the King and *work* for what I want. The King is salvation for my spirit and work is salvation for my soul. When I choose the King, I get everything that goes with Him—some *act-right*, success, and joy!

Blind to Spiritual Abuse

Roni church leaders most often lead Ronies to worship them, not God. Those leaders do this for money, power, and to be served rather than to serve. These HRIC's do not teach us what the Bible says nor do they live exemplary lives—according to Bible teachings. They tell us to listen to them and not to God. They teach us to do what they say to do, but not as they do. They teach us to follow them even when they are living like the devil. They take God's seat and point us toward themselves. We are

106

blind because we want to be convinced that it is okay to do wrong. They give us an excuse to act like Roni. Roni-makers don't go to doctors who are *just*-a-man; they go to specialists who are skillful and liable for malpractice. Yet, Ronies continue to follow a Roni-preacher who is *just-a-man*. People are neither willing to have a heart transplant by someone who is *just-a-man*, nor have brain surgery by a doctor who just happens to be *merely human*. So, why would you have your soul lead by a preacher, who is also *just-a-man, indecent, and broke*?

Roni-preachers also teach us untrue, ugly and nasty things about who we are. They infiltrate our minds with negative rhetoric, "You are filthy rags." The Bible does not mean that we are filthy rags but that our righteous is like filthy rags because we cannot earn salvation. Salvation is not the result of anything that we can do; it is by the grace of God in Christ. However, our salvation will result in doing what is right. Good works don't save us but if we are saved we will do good works. But calling us filthy

> OUR FEEL-GOOD PREACHERS TELL US HOW LOW-DOWN WE ARE AND TEACH US TO BE LOW-DOWN.

rags is mean, abusive, and shame/fear based Roni-theology. They tell us we are hell bound, downtrodden, and without a chance, helpless over sin, and that we cannot act right on our own because we don't have an ounce of goodness in us. So, they teach us that we cannot help ourselves against bad-acting because we are all bad. But we like this because it makes us feel good about acting wrongly. Our feel-good preachers tell us how low-down we are and teach us to be low-down. They say, "We aren't any better than nobody else," to discourage us from striving to live a life free from wrongdoing. They say, "I've learned more from doing wrong than from doing right," to teach us to be a fool by learning the hard way instead of learning from knowledge. They compare us to other people rather than comparing us to the King.

We are responsible for who we follow. After all, it is our choice and it is our souls to save. We can let ourselves be fooled but need not be shocked when God says to us in the judgment, "I never knew you!"

Most so-called Roni *preachers* are merely narcissists with low self-esteem. They do not have a clue that you cannot bring people up when you are lower than they are. Even when they attend accredited seminaries that teach responsible and righteous living, they do not communicate these values to the people who follow them. When our Roni preachers go to accredited seminaries, they walk in front of the White folks to get their degrees, but when they return to preach and teach us, the front wears off and they go back to being the Ronies they are and give us a Roni-theology of ignorance and disorder—N-word Theology. It is time for Roni preachers to stop faking and fronting to get the White-man's college and seminary degrees only to return to our churches with the same old Roni-making fake-gospel.

> IT IS TIME FOR RONI PREACHERS TO STOP FAKING AND FRONTING TO GET THE WHITE-MAN'S SEMINARY DEGREES ONLY TO RETURN TO OUR CHURCHES WITH THE SAME OLD RONI-MAKING FAKE-GOSPEL.

We show up in the White-accredited schools to get an education. That's not the problem. The problem is that we front and fake to get it and don't use it. We put on a front to get the degrees and when it all said and done we fail to transmit knowledge to our own people. Contrarily, I accepted education a different way. I saw it as my way out of poverty, and not only sought to get the letters behind my name, but to get the knowledge that came with the letters. Thus, my education helped me, unlike the Ronies who cheat, scheme, and sleep around to get by and get a grade they don't deserve.

WE DON'T TEACH WHAT IS GOOD FOR OUR PEOPLE

We refuse to transmit and teach what we know is better for our people. We would rather make ourselves kings and have our own group of slaves than to give freedom to our people. Knowledge is the pathway to freedom. Just as racism is terrorism, so is self-sustained ignorance. Putting knowledge into practice allows us to live in freedom, but we would rather enslave and be slaves. Those who have knowledge, but refuse to share it suppress others for their own gain. Do not let those leaders fool you. If your preacher condemns, belittles and degrades you, wake up! The chains may be invisible, but they are wrapped around your spirit. Seek knowledge of God yourself and stop relying on the preacher, then you will find your path to freedom. These false preachers use the pulpit as a platform for comedy, news casting, political agendas, to glory in the depravity of their lives before they supposedly came to Christ, and to engage in sports team praise. They show us all of the bad things that we are and emulate them before their congregations. What they do a little of we do on a larger scale, because, after all, they are in charge, so they must be right. Sadly, this kind of thinking allows the blind to continue leading the blind.

> WE WOULD RATHER MAKE OURSELVES KINGS AND HAVE OUR OWN GROUP OF SLAVES THAN TO GIVE FREEDOM TO OUR PEOPLE.

It is supposed to be a *pulpit* not a *pushpit,* pushing us into foolishness instead of righteousness. Consequently, nobody is accountable and nobody is getting any better because of these so-called spiritual and community leaders. HRIC's on the TV calling themselves workers of the vision of Martin Luther King, only help us to be unaccountable for our actions and teach us to feel sorry for ourselves when we are wrong. This is especially sad among my people because *we* need the truth more than anyone in order to get us out of the pit we are in. When I realized how I'd been manipulated, lied to, and tricked in Roni-dom, I thought my people must be cursed. But then I understood that although *we* may be cursed collectively as a group based on what our Noah descendants did (*Genesis 9:22-26*)[17], we are not cursed individually when we submit to the King; the King took away the curse from those who do not choose to be Roni. I did not fall into the predispositions of my forefathers or my background because I walked with the King. We need some act-right and we need Jesus more than anyone.

Let me be clear about a curse. A curse does not apply to those who follow the way of Christ and dwell in Him, but when we look at how we are faring in the world, there is good reason to believe that there is some validity to this curse theory. Yet, we have a way out when we accept the one who removed all curses--Jesus Christ. But even if I am not walking

> EVEN IF I AM NOT WALKING WITH THE KING, I DO NOT DESERVE TO BE TERRORIZED AND MURDERED.

with the King, I don't deserve to be terrorized and murdered; I deserve to be loved and taught by instruction and example.

So, regarding "Blindness," we can *see* if we want to see because of God's grace. But if we want to be blind, we have plenty of help from our so-called leaders, our new slave owners. However, being blind to what is right does not keep us from paying the cost for blindness in our wrongdoing. We must wake-up; in the end we will be held accountable for every idle word and deed. Wake up now, rather than later. Godspeed with this!

---

[17] **22**Ham, the father of Canaan, saw his father naked and told his two brothers outside. **23**But Shem and Japheth took a garment and laid it across their shoulders; then they walked in backward and covered their father's naked body. Their faces were turned the other way so that they would not see their father naked. **24**When Noah awoke from his wine and found out what his youngest son had done to him, **25**he said," Cursed be Canaan! The lowest of slaves will he be to his brothers." **26**He also said, "Praise be to the LORD, the God of Shem! May Canaan be the slave of Shem (Genesis 9:22-26; NIV).

Also…Romans 13:1-5, reminds us to…

Let every person be subject to the governing authorities. For there is no authority except from God, and those that exist have been instituted by God. Therefore whoever resists the authorities resists what God has appointed, and those who resist will incur judgment. For rulers are not a terror to good conduct, but to bad. Would you have no fear of the one who is in authority? Then do what is good, and you will receive his approval, for he is God's servant for your good. But if you do wrong, be afraid, for he does not bear the sword in vain. For he is the servant of God, an avenger who carries out God's wrath on the wrongdoer. Therefore one must be in subjection, not only to avoid God's wrath but also for the sake of conscience (ESV).

As for standard, the church, the state, media,
and our leaders teach us there is no standard
because there is no requirement for the
demonstration *of the virtues we say we believe.*
Ex: a bad-actor is deemed good without the demonstration of what is good. Ex: America goes
for propaganda of making America great again,
when America was great when we were slaves
and this is supposed to be good? This lawlessness
and recklessness, is not good or great! Therefore,
when there is no difference between right
and wrong, no difference between who we are
and what we are called and call ourselves,
and when what is right is made to
be wrong and what is wrong is made to be
right ....and when there is no law because
the law protects the lawless, rich, and white supremacists....then nothing matters........
for any individual or group...... not even life.
And then our only result is utter destruction!

Chapter 7   Relearning: Teach Your Children This and Save Their Lives!

At first, because I was blind, I unknowingly acted like Roni. I had learned some faulty things. The first faulty idea I learned was that *nothing matters*. This caused me to be aloof and absent in my own life. This is wrong, because *things do matter*. I matter—*the first thing* I had to learn about was about myself.

What I relearned about myself

Making a choice to act like Roni is one thing; acting without knowing that I am acting like Roni is another. We must always be in charge of what we are doing by owning it, because we alone will have to pay for it. So if I don't want to pay for something, I must not do that something.

However, acting like Roni is not always bad. Some people do not understand anything but Roni. In isolated and special cases, it may be beneficial to know how to act like Roni, but I try to avoid these situations because they can lead to someone not going home, especially when Roni is violent. Therefore, we must know how to survive in Roniville until we can relocate out and away from it.

I learned other bad things about myself that cause non-Ronies to think all people who look like me are Ronies. These are some of the problems Ronies present to society:

- You can't be nice to certain people—ones like me—because if you are, I will run all over you and try to tell you what to do. I try to run things and people that I have no control over. I try to make the rules when *I don't own nothin' and ain't in charge of nothin'*.

- I don't know what "stop" and "no" mean. So I don't get it until someone is provoked into insulting, threatening, beating, or killing me.
- I don't know when to stop talking. So I "spill the beans" on myself and act like I don't know why I have problems.
- I cannot change—while I am Roni, because I don't want to do right, don't want to pay for doing wrong, and blame something and someone outside of myself for my troubles. I won't ever change because I cannot change while I am Roni.
- And worst of all, I become a target because I look like I am a threat to society.

THE SIX SIMPLE LESSONS FOR SUCCESS

1. Close my mouth
2. Sit down and stay still
3. Pay attention/Stand at attention/ Eyes on the teacher & task
4. Follow Instructions
5. Keep my mouth and hands to myself, off people and things that do not belong to me
6. Complete the job/work by staying on task

(T.1)

Sadly, for a longtime, I would not follow instructions. Until now, I could not follow instructions because my Roni parents would take-up for me when I was wrong. Because my parents did not teach me, I did not learn the Six Simple Lessons (T.1) that would make me successful until later in life. I learned them the hard way through hard times, pain and suffering, but I learned them. Then the other seven completed me in being successful and happy.

THE THIRTEEN LESSONS TO MY SUCCESS

Add the six simple lessons to the remaining seven, and you have thirteen lessons (T.2) that can decrease and even halt American racist terrorism against all of us. By living according to these Thirteen Lessons, we will regain our resilience and self-respect. I am often given the opportunity to teach children who do not have parents to teach them. I say to them, "I'm sorry that your parents have not taught you and you've not had the opportunity to have good home training; so I'm going to teach you what you have not learned (the Six Lessons)."

> WE CANNOT CONTINUE TO EXCUSE STUDENTS FROM ACTING RIGHT BECAUSE THEY HAVE NOT HAD PROPER HOME TRAINING.

We cannot continue to excuse students from acting right because they have not had proper home training. We can teach them at school and church by having a zero tolerance for their failure to demonstrate these Six Lessons. Then we can help them to reach success by teaching them all Thirteen Lessons. We must require the Six Lessons in all structured settings—the home, church, school, work. And stop justifying us not insisting on children abiding by these Six Lessons by saying, "It begins at home."

THE THIRTEEN LESSONS TO MY SUCCESS (T.2)

1. **Close my mouth**
2. **Sit down and stay still**
3. **Pay attention/Stand at attention (keep eyes on teacher/task)**
4. **Follow Instructions**
5. **Keep my mouth and hands to myself—off of other people and things that don't belong to me**
6. **Complete the job/work/task by staying on task.**

7. **Stay Visible:** Do not go where you are not known. Stay in familiar surroundings and carry a cell phone with you so that anytime to call 911 for police assistance with White lawmen, bullies, etc.

8. **Be Calm:** Do not resist (don't try to pull your body away or make any sudden moves. Speak when you are spoken to and say, 'Yes Sir," "Yes Ma'am," "Please," and "Thank you."

9. **Talk Right:** Do not talk back. Do not question the bully-cop. Do not dispute his/her claims.

10. **Look Right:** Do not make a mean face or express anger on your face. Keep a pleasant expression, but do not laugh or smile. Make eye contact with authority figures but do not stare.

11. **Know What They Think:** Understand how the world views us: Never equal, must be better (work harder and not react or take offense to insults or mistreatment); we will be the last hired first fired, not receive equal pay for equal work; and that since we are black we are seen as N.........

12. **Act Right:** Correct our Behavior as not to fulfill racial stereotypes and to demonstrate the character of a law-abiding and contributing member of society—an American Taxpaying Citizen.

13. **Be Right:** Be a Christ-follower in word and deed, so that we may be wise in the world, gain the favor of God and man, follow peace with everyone, and be kind to everyone at all times—a Christian.

I can't understand the countless times speakers in the church have reveled in saying, "It begins at home!" Yes! Training should start at home, but the problem is that it cannot begin at home when *parents* have not been trained. Still, this has nothing to do with what structured environments (churches, schools, social clubs, civil organization, sports leagues, prison/jail systems, all social systems) can do to insist on these lessons. Children who want to be included will practice these Six Lessons, but we cannot let them stay if they will not obey.

Otherwise, we reward wrong behavior and teach them that they can get what they want without doing what it takes to get it. They are not getting it at home, so why don't we make them get it at school and church? There must be a zero tolerance policy for violations of these rules if we want to save our children and ourselves from American racism, bigotry, and from our own self-hatred.

I am teaching Roni to obey the teacher who is me right now! *"If ain't nobody ever taught you anything, this is your chance to learn by doing what I am telling you."* These are rules to follow with everyone and in every situation. Targets of society, especially, must follow these rules when we in the custody of so-called lawmen because many of them are lawless and are looking for an opportunity to demonstrate their hatred of us. Don't give them the opportunity to injure, badger, or even kill you. Showing good manners demonstrates that you have respect for authority.

In addition to the previously listed Six Lessons you must also learn seven additional lessons, totaling Thirteen Lessons that will help us to defeat disadvantage, injury, and injustice:

7. Stay Visible: Do not go where you are not known. Stay in familiar surroundings and carry a cell phone with you so that anytime a White lawman (police, sheriff, highway patrolman, constable, etc.) pulls you over in a car, or stops you, you can *call the police on the police-call 911; put your phone on speaker and place it out of your hands.* This will give you a better chance of not being killed by a bully-lawman who has stopped, apprehended, or cornered you.

8. Be Calm: Do not resist (don't try to pull your body away or make any sudden moves; don't show a bad-facial attitude). Speak when you are spoken to and say, "Yes, Sir," "Yes, Ma'am," "Please," and "Thank you." Cooperate with the cops because you don't know when you will run into an egotistical bully who might shoot/kill or injure you on purpose (or accidentally). Make no sudden moves. We know this doesn't always work and some of them will kill/shoot us anyway.

9. Talk Right: Do not talk back. Do not question the bully-cop. Do not dispute his/her claims. Express agreement and agree quickly considering him/her a potential enemy.[18] ***DO NOT PUT YOUR HANDS IN YOUR POCKETS, DON'T POINT, DON'T MAKE HAND GESTURES OR SHOW A BAD ATTITUDE!***

10. Look Right: Do not make a mean face or express anger on your face. Keep a pleasant expression, but do not laugh or smile. Make eye contact with authority figures but do not stare. Always dress clean, neat, modestly--to cover everything private and keep your pants up!

The ten lessons above are what we must do individually. Then collectively we must achieve the remaining three to total thirteen lessons:

11. Know What They Think: Understand how the world views us: Never equal, must be better (work harder and not react or take offense to insults or mistreatment); we will be the last hired first fired, not receive equal pay for equal work; and that since we are black we are seen as N—, etc. Thus, we must know who we are in God, i.e., a representative of the King, and therefore a royal priesthood.

12. Act Right: Correct our behavior as not to fulfill racial stereotypes and to demonstrate the character of a law-abiding and

---

[18] Agree with your adversary quickly, while you are on the way with him, lest your adversary deliver you to the judge, the judge hand you over to the officer, and you be thrown into prison (Matthew 5:25 NKJV).

contributing member of society—an American Taxpaying Citizen—NOT an African anything!

13. Be Right: Be a Christ-follower in word and deed, so that we may be wise in the world, gain the favor of God and man, follow peace with everyone, and be kind to everyone at all times—a Christian.

Living by these principles will help us to establish justice and correct our identity. Then we won't look like ALL of us are bad-actors. Now.... doing right doesn't always mean that we will not be wronged or killed as did Rev. Martin Luther King, Jr., but most of us will not be MLK's or Job's. Therefore, we can reasonably expect to be treated as we should when we do abide by these Thirteen Lessons, except those who are picked out to be picked on for God's glory—for which God gives you an elevator to take you up.

Failure to learn to live by these thirteen guidelines has caused many of us to be poor, injured, locked up, diseased, and killed. We didn't learn how to close our mouths; so we get in fights with each other over nothing and get beat up and killed by law enforcement officers. We didn't learn to keep our hands to ourselves and we go around touching things that don't belong to us. We put our hands on other people and on things we cannot buy. Our bad-acting parents never taught us to *look, but don't touch.* So, it is easy for us to steal. We play with things that don't belong to us in stores and our stupid-acting parents do nothing. When we get in trouble—fighting and stealing—neither we nor our parents know we've caused our trouble.

WHY KEEP YOUR HANDS AND MOUTHS TO YOURSELF?

Our parents never taught us how to treat others and how to respect other folks stuff. We never learned *don't touch* what doesn't belong to you. We don't know the difference between touching, borrowing, and stealing. Roni-parents never taught us to respect and obey authority. They let us do and say whatever we wanted to do and say. They tell us to stop without enforcing that we stop. They do this because they don't want to be bothered with us. Instead of providing guidance, our parents have temper tantrums when we make them mad. They have no real commitment to teaching by example—probably because they didn't have an example either; but this is no excuse. Everybody has known what is right even if think they have forgotten due to doing wrong so long until they have made themselves believe they are right. Sadly, people without a moral compass teach

> DISREGARD FOR THE THIRTEEN PRINCIPLES IS KILLING US.

children to act badly. At first, they think our bad-acting is cute, but what is cute when you are a three-year-old is fatal for a seventeen-year-old. One wrong move of nonverbal provocation to a fool with a gun can cause the senseless death of a young person, especially young Ronies.

Society does not know the difference between a Black law-abiding citizen contributing to society and a Black-Roni. So, they are set to kill us all. Disregard for *The Thirteen Principles* is killing us. If we will *sit still, close our mouths, and pay attention* we can learn these principles—but we must listen. Since we think the rules don't matter, when the police say, "Stand at attention with your hands to your side," and you put your hands in your pockets, what do you think the policeman might do? He might shoot you thinking that you have a weapon in your pockets. Remember he is already terrified of us. So, these rules are essential to our survival. We must return to what we know is the way—like our forefathers taught us. When we fail to follow these rules, we look as though we are resisting arrest, and some of us *do* resist arrest, talk noise, and show disrespect to police officers. Most of what we do to provoke bullies is going against what *Mama and Big Mama* taught us, which is *"do not talk back, do not point, do not stare, do not raise your voice, do not roll your eyes, do not display your disgust/anger/indifference, don't run from me, and do not raise your hands/arms when I'm talking to you."*

Since we did not allow our parents, teachers, and grandparents to teach us these lessons—or we did not have parents or grandparents, we do not know how to act. Then the legal-wrongdoers will teach us the wrong way. We are too enmeshed into the lies that make us think we have arrived. Yes, we've come a long way, but we have a long, long way to go. We are accidents and fatalities waiting to happen because no one has taught us to act right and we are not held accountable for our actions. We think excuses are reasons enough, so there is no need to obey the rules. But... Big Mama said, "ALL EXCUSES ARE LIES!" Ronies and Non-Ronies who have learned these six lessons (T.1, page 113) are in a better position to avoid the abuse of the law by obeying the law because we respect authority.

> WE NEED TO STOP TERRORIZING AMERICA AND AMERICA NEEDS TO STOP TERRORIZING US.

Too many of us are forever learning, but never coming into the full knowledge of truth; because we make excuses, that are nothing but lies; then we fool ourselves believing our own lies. Tragically, God will let us believe our lies if that's what we want and when this happens we cannot even hear God. When the state punishes us for our wrongdoing, we will not be around to teach our children The Thirteen Principles and then the cycle will continue from generation to generation.

They will kill our children for—talking back, pointing, staring, raising their voices, rolling eyes, displaying anger, shrugging their feet, running away, showing facial anger or a bad attitude, or raising their arms. In my youth, we'd get a beating if we did any of these things. Now, we let ourselves get tricked by the empty promises of integration. We are afraid of the police and the police are afraid of us. This *mutual fear* causes a reaction from both sides. And now the war is on! We flee in fear and the police fire on us out of fear—sometimes resulting in cold-blooded murder.

We need to stop terrorizing America and America needs to stop terrorizing us. America has turned on all of us because nobody knows the difference between Black and Roni. Now we are firing back because the guns Caesar gave America to hold us at bay are now in our hands to fire back on the one who started firing at us.

We have put ourselves further behind the starting line than from whence we first started.

We can be the bigger of the two terrors and start to heal the Black-White American Divide. I am appealing to us because I believe we have the fortitude, strength, and humility to make the first move although we were the first wronged.

We could demonstrate and learn how to act if we will listen to and obey our teachers. No need to tell us that training starts at home, when there is no one at home to train us.

Try it this way; hear it from the young person we are discussing:

"You (pastors, teachers, group leaders, coaches, criminal justice systems) just train me in the way I should go when I am in your face and when I am in your place. Since my parents didn't teach me, at least I will have gotten proper training from somebody--YOU! Problem is I didn't learn at home and you let me slip and slide by in school, on the job, and at the church, until I was dismissed in shock cause you rewarded my wrong behavior, so now I'm old (not grown) and stupid because I never learned how to act. My teachers who teach the right way are called bad names and disrespected because Ronies have no respect for authority, no respect for doing the right thing or for obeying the law or God. We are a walking threat to society because we have never learned the Six Lessons when we were children. My parents didn't teach me these Six Lessons and wouldn't let my teachers teach me these Six Lessons either; so now I don't know how to act and nobody wants to fool with me. I'm nothing but bullet bait for the police because I act stupid and threatening.

I learn how to look like a target at home and at church because inept youth matrons, preachers, and teachers let me get up and mumble out those stupid Easter speeches, playing with my hands, fumbling with my fingers, shuffling my feet while I'm speaking, and looking stupid all upside the walls and floor. Poor teaching doesn't know that perfect practice makes perfect and improper practices makes improper. My untrained teachers taught me to act improperly. When the police see me this way, they are afraid of me and don't know what I am going to do with my hands; so they shoot me by accident but I am no less dead all because I didn't learn Six Lessons from my parents and teachers. Now, I'm old (not grown because grown is on your own), I don't want to know how to act even if my parents didn't teach me because I have no respect for authority or education. I could learn how to act—it's a matter of obeying the teacher, but I won't because my dumb-acting parents disrespected the teacher (right in front of me) and took up for me when I was wrong.

I don't know how to act for two reasons: (1) I go against what I know is right and have made my conscience as hard as a rock; and (2) I justify my bad-acts by making up lies to excuse my bad acts. I made this double-dose bullet against myself that has made me believe my own lies; so I've lied to myself and don't even know it. I live in **Don'tEvenNoIAmLying** (to myself), and feel victimized by my own hard-heart and blinded eyes.

Sadly, there are so many of our racial group who behave badly, until people and the police perhaps unknowingly think all us are bad. And what we do on TV certainly makes it look like all of us are bad-actors-- public fighting, stealing, teasing, taunting, dancing and loud-talking in public, coming out of the house improperly dressed, airing your dirty low-down ways on national TV. I have experienced this perception from white folks and lawmen, that all of us are N— (lazy, broke, bad-actors, trying to get something for free).

For example, I have an insurance policy for medications that has no co-pay for me, but when I go into Walgreens Pharmacy the staff treat me like I am a poor, crazy, N-Word trying to get something for free when my insurance company is open 24 hours and can be verified and approved. They are getting paid, but think of me as getting something for free when I earned the benefit. What would cause the staff to look at me and not at my insurance information right on their computer? It's that they see a Roni when they see the color of my skin. This is the only answer I can come up with as to why they are treating me like I'm an N—. As a Roni look-a-like, I get treated wrongly because some people think all individuals in my racial group are Ronies. All of us are not Ronies because Ronies come in all colors, but bigots and racists who are in positions of authority want to think all people who look alike are alike, providing them an excuse to hate and injure people in the name of law and order and Christianity, when it's not about law and order or about Jesus. It's about their hatred, abuse, and racism against me and I suffer it although I am not the one who helped to bring it on. I tell racists that I am not a nigger and don't appreciate being treated as if I am one. If they get offended, but they stop treating me like one, then I say, tell them!"

INSTITUTIONAL RACISM & WHITE PRIVILEGE

Institutional Racism & White Privilege (an elevated status that guards against racism and due process of law). White privilege spills over into industry and heightens institutional racism. These cruel realities are our real enemies. We are still wrongly treated as a race through a minimum wage that is not enough for us to survive and through unequal employment practices. Sadly, white supremacists run major companies and we still are not given equal pay for equal work although we are oftentimes more qualified. Institutional Racism seems to be felt by middle class blacks who excel in higher education to a greater extent than ever. Racist beliefs are herald throughout the media and there is no shame. Our young people are hearing this and are going to jobs that they've earned college degrees for and are not getting the same pay as their white counterparts. This is discouraging and hurtful to them and this is tragic. This is the greatest detriment of the view that all black people are N—. It may be that the majority of us are not striving for the American dream of home ownership, higher education, and white-collar careers, but still the ALL effect is hurting even the innocent black young people who are hard workers and high achievers. They too are targets of wrongful collateral damage.

There is a great deal of hopelessness and apathy among the young because they seem to be in a no-win situation whether they do what is wrong or right. They don't know when they are to obey their superiors or when not. To "rightly obey" means to obey those in-charge when what they are telling you to do is not wrong. On the other hand, if someone in charge tells you to do something that is bad or wrong, you must then *tell it* until somebody listens. Otherwise, we are to obey and do as we are told because those who teach us to do what is right are doing so to help and protect us. Authority is of God and we must operate under authority so that we may operate with authority (Rom 13).

Bad-acting so-called lawmen get away with killing us by discrediting us by our bad-acts. When they do this they are abusing the authority that God approves. They justify killing, abusing, and injuring us by pointing out our bad-acting and try to make society forget that they kill us for no *good* reason. All of this goes back to our bad-acts and their racism. If we don't give the police a reason to justify killing us, America would put a stop to this brutality. If we give the police no reason or way to justify killing us they could not keep getting away with killing Ronies and Roni look-a-likes. We all know it's not everyone, but when there are so many more who act bad that look alike, it makes it look like everybody (of our race) is a Roni, especially to those who want to have an excuse to hate people based on the way they look.

No or Poor Home Training Created Me:

I didn't learn until later in life—after a screwed up over and over again—that it all starts with home training. My bad-acting parents dress me up so that I looked good, but they never saw to it that I behaved well. I was *dressed up and messed up* and often hungry. Often I lacked sleep. The television was my babysitter teaching me to live up to the stereotypes of Ronies—killing one another, stealing, being loud, lazy, and disrespectful, like it was normal. Although my bad-acting parents sent me to school, they did not want teachers to say anything to me about my behavior.

They sent me to church and did not want the people in charge to correct me. I made everyone in charge not want to fool with me, so I was passed along from grade to grade and from room to room, but never learned anything. I thought I was getting by because I got my way, but I got nothing but stupidity and ignorance that put me in danger of catching bullets. Now I feel totally unaccountable for my actions and don't know how to act. Does this sound familiar to you? Can you identify with my experience?

COSTLY NOTHING DEGREES

No one in my world holds the line on right and wrong, not the church, not the school, not the state, and certainly not the media, because they just want to make money by making Roni look for pies-in-the-sky instead of getting an education and working. Real Roni-dummies have made an entire economic system from getting *nothing* degrees, so we end up getting degrees that cost more than we can make only because we want the easy way out. Many do not want to do what it takes to get a *real* education. Oh, yes, there are many of us with *paper*, but too many of us with the *paper* have not been educated. There is no impartation of knowledge that is a modification of behavior. Consequently, without the demonstration of a change there is no evidence of an education.

The educational system knows that we won't let them educate us when we are young; so, we don't have what it takes. This has created all kinds of useless colleges and schools that charge a lot of money, leading to big educational loans for those who have no prospect for job placement. We have the nerve to say, "I got an education, but can't get a good job," when we have a *nothing degree* that provides no opportunities for significant employment.

Fact is, if the school, college, or university is not regionally accredited by the Council for Higher Education (CHEA) (and you can search this site),[19] you must understand that you won't be able to get a job with the degree in many companies in the secular/academic world. Some schools listed are accredited to grant degrees in the state they are located in but not regionally accredited. We (Black folks) are prime victims of nothing degrees. Check CHEA before you get a nothing degree. Demand and supply are still an economic reality!

> BLACK FOLKS ARE PRIME VICTIMS OF WORTHLESS DEGREES, SO CHECK CHEA BEFORE YOU GET A "NOTHING" DEGREE.

And then when you do get a degree, make sure that it is a degree that you can get a job in—think of demand and supply. We haven't realized that we need to go to school to be nurses, doctors, lawyers, dentists, dental assistants, medical assistants, medical technicians, barbers, certified teachers, academically trained ministers/pastors/preachers, hair stylists, academically trained musicians, and other hands-on and public-service educationally prepared professionals.

For the best job availability, you must not put all your eggs in one basket but use your HANDS, HEART and HEAD.

- HAND: Use what is in your hands (cleaning, cooking, serving, ironing, sewing, babysitting, etc)

[19] Search CHEA (Council for Higher Education Accreditation @ [http://chea.org/search/search.asp?flag=1] Retrieved May 24, 2016.

- HEART: Train yourself to provide a product or service from your heart—helping, yard work, decorating, sewing, baking, etc.
- HEAD: Educate yourself to provide a service that only those who are trained can do: nursing, school teacher, accountant, engineer, technician, OT, PT, speech therapist, court reporter, etc.

Since we don't want to put in what it takes to be successful, we end up getting dumb-Roni degrees that cost large sums of money—money that we cannot earn back in the field we've studied in—Leadership, Organizational Management, Christian Ministry. Who does that? Dumb-Ronies! We know nothing about and care nothing about getting terminal degrees or about supply and demand. We act so stupid until we create more problems for ourselves in life—socially, secularly, and spiritually. Education for dumb-Ronies is the new cash cow and the state and federal government are *racking it up* from the dummies that have *nothing degrees*.

At the same time, I don't understand what is going on within our culture group. The rest of us who have not gotten trapped neck-deep in student loans—that we will never be able to pay off—keep getting killed as collateral damage and put in jail without any idea of our own accountability. (For the most part, I caused what happened to me because my lack of knowledge and poor upbringing). Our failure to educate ourselves the right way causes us to be unable to survive. Education is now a racket and the cash cow against poor people. You must get a QUALITY education; not just any kind of education. Since education is the only way to success, the lack thereof is the secondary way of killing us, other than outright killing us with bullets, knives, and capital punishment.

APPROVAL OF KILLING US WRONGLY

America will not and almost cannot afford to punish those who kill us wrongly, because right now putting Roni in jail or killing Roni is thought to be the only way to keep Roni at bay. Everyone is terrified of Roni. I know I am, even though I would not kill Roni like *throwed-off* bully-cops who think all of us are the same. These cops kill Roni, kill anybody who looks like Roni, and then think we'll be done with Roni. God forbid! This can change if we get some *act-right* within our group. We appear to be the worst of all bad-actors such that we make it hard for all of us. This is all about social order—what every civilized and thriving society must maintain.

ROOTS OF REBELLION

My bad-acting parents taught me to disrespect authority figures in school, in the community, and at church, not realizing they've set me up to be defamed and killed by authority figures with badges, guns, hatred, and clubs. I've torn up the schools, so the teachers couldn't teach me or the other children for that matter. Now, that I've been schooled the hard way—finding out the consequences of my actions through experience—I've realized I was wrong. I got away with acting a fool because it was easier to do what I felt instead of what I knew to be right.

The children who wanted to learn couldn't because I was so disruptive, the teacher spent most of her time chastising and correcting my bad-acting behavior. Sometimes I had learning and behavioral problems that required help, but most of the time I was just acting badly. The teachers and the doctors couldn't distinguish BAD from ADD and ADHD; so they labeled me with a sickness to help justify my bad-acting. Instead of helping me, the diagnosis gave *me* an excuse to misbehave. I never learned—until later in life—that the reason doesn't make it okay.

The reason was to help me to change, not to help me stay the same. My lazy-acting parents only wanted me to have a diagnosis of ADD and ADHD and all other kind of alphabets so they could get a check to spend on themselves and their boyfriend and girlfriends. They did nothing to raise me right so I could act right. Instead, I caused trouble everywhere I went—at home, church, and school and my parents protected me when I am wrong.

SCHOOL TEACHERS AND THE REST OF US
Teacher Abuse

Thus gifted teachers left leaving us with teachers who were worse than Ronies—dummies, child molesters, pedophiles, alcoholics, drug addicts, and criminals; those became our teachers. The state didn't pay enough to have anyone credible to stay around to teach us, and the state took away the teachers' authority. Teachers were given responsibility without being given authority. To make matters worse, the teachers were blamed for our bad-acting. The state blamed the teachers for what we did; so neither us nor our bad-acting parents accepted responsibility for any of the wrong on our part, although we willfully committed wrong acts. Further making matters worse, the state punished parents and teachers who tried to help us. The state punishes parents for spanking their children who need it and they punish the teachers who try to teach us. Then policemen kill us for the same behavior our parents and teachers tried to prevent with spanking and training—their hands were tied.

Why obey the teacher? Any good teacher says to students, ***"I am the only teacher who counts in this room right now; so you sit down and listen to me and do what I say and do it right now!"*** But we lose these good teachers who think this way and we make them feel that they are wrong for taking their rightful authority. Students are allowed to think that the teacher is responsible for their bad-acting selves. They take advantage of the teachers who are nice (as if they are sponges), but listen in fear to teachers whom they think are strict (bricks). But no matter if your teacher acts like a brick or a sponge, children must respect them if they was to learn. Our parents leave us no room to learn anything at home, at school, at church, or in the community. So, on one hand there were parents who turned their backs on their kids and there were parents who are punished for trying to discipline their kids. This is a no-win situation. We don't have a chance other than to act right ourselves and it's hard to raise yourself when you don't know how to act.

Parents and State Against Teachers

Bad-acting parents and the bad-acting state help us to disrespect authority by insulting our teachers right in front of us and blaming them for our nonperformance. We know they are not to blame, but we like putting the blame on someone else and getting by; they have made Ronies out of all of us students regardless of our race, creed or kind. We have no respect or love for ourselves or others. Teachers can't correct us, they can't punish us, and they can't put us out. They have nothing to work with to get us to act right and our parents don't help them. Teachers, who do care, get targeted, wrongly scandalized, and ousted from their jobs. So, it's best for teachers to, "Walk the policy, do their job, and not demonstrate love to Roni-students, because if they do, they'll be targeted and end up broke, like the unlovely, and unloving Ronies they wasted their time on.

Teachers, Save Yourselves

Teachers! Do the job as written and walk on out the door with your paycheck. Roni-students *ain't* worth the trouble and neither are their bad-acting parents. To heck with all of them! Nobody can prove a teacher is not doing his or her job if they do it by the book and not by the heart. Putting your heart into Roni is reckless for you because you cannot teach students who do not want to learn. Remember, **you can take a horse to water but you can't make him drink, and you can send a child to school but you can't make him think**.

Ronies don't want to learn and don't want anybody else to learn, anyway. So, students who want to learn must rely upon *reading for themselves* as a way of self-teaching. Teachers' ability to teach has been taken away by bad-acting parents, students, and a government that blames them for how other bad actors carry on. This destruction of schooling happened because right and wrong are treated the same and blamed on someone other than the one who is acting badly. I tear up the job the same way that I've torn up the schools. So, I keep all the other employees from working like I did the other students from learning so I won't have to do anything at work or school. When I flunk out of school or get fired, I never know why and think they have done me wrong! If I would have listened to my good parents and teachers, I would have avoided this trouble.

DISGRACE BY OUR OWN MOUTHS

Learning how to close your mouth is very beneficial. Our modern times have provided individuals an opportunity to *act out* for the entire world to see largely because we won't close our mouths. Ronies are destroying and disgracing themselves on social media. Nobody taught Roni to keep your business to yourself and to keep your big mouth shut?

Eighty percent of Ronies in jail told on themselves. *Caesar didn't have no evidence, but Roni never learned to shut his mouth!* When we get into trouble, we don't even know what we've done to cause harm to ourselves because we have no self-control and no conscience. We certainly can't figure out a way to get out of trouble. So, we keep on doing the same things while looking for different results—dumb! We blame situations on things and people outside of ourselves; then we walk around with a target on our backs by failing to *close our mouths, sit still, pay attention, follow instructions, keep our hands to ourselves, and complete the job/task—which adds up to me not respecting authority.* Can you believe I have the nerve to be shocked about getting a dart in my back? Then, I blame everybody and everything else instead of owning my choices.

You Can Turn It Around!

After I had learned to act like Roni, I cried to my Big Mama saying, "They've all turned against me because of the family lies my Roni-parents told to discredit me; nobody likes me and the teachers are mean to me." She said to me, "Don't worry about what nobody else is doing; you just do the right thing and God will bless you." "But Big Mama, the teachers won't teach me; they are listening to the lies and they hate me," I said. She answered, "Can you read? Can you learn everything in those old books? Look, Baby, nobody has to be nice to you and nobody has to teach you because a book doesn't hate anybody. Don't worry about what they are doing and you do what you're supposed to do and God will bless you!"

Big Mama taught me to become my own teacher. She knew if I focused on myself, I'd have more than enough time to forget everybody else and do what it takes to become financially and emotionally independent. Big Mama gave

> We need to stop looking at what THEY are doing, and look at what WE are doing.

me freedom from Roni by pointing me to loving God. It took me to realize what Big Mama was trying to get me to understand. Later, her words rang in my ear and I realized that I had to teach myself to get ahead in Roni-dom. A good education was my way out of poverty and abuse, but one thing is for sure you can't learn anything while looking around at everything and everybody and tending to everyone else's business, but your own because your mind goes where your eyes go.

Where was I looking?

I guess I was looking at everything that had happened to me—my past—and what everybody else was doing because I didn't learn what Big Mama taught me at first and I struggled with Roni-dom while being Roni—tending to everyone else's business except my own, trying to prove something to Ronies who didn't matter, and trying to undo something that only God could undo. I was mad and I didn't even know it.

A Rough Start But Eventually A Smooth Finish

Since I didn't want to work through my problems, at first, I just started *trouble* everywhere I'd go. Starting fights with people, talking about people, putting others down, talking bad about co-workers, conspiring against them to get them ridiculed or fired, telling vicious lies and being messy to keep from working and being messy on the job got me fired, but I still kept on bringing mess—talking against my boss on Face book and to other people who'd go back and tell the boss what I'd said against them.

Telling my business on social media caused me social and legal problems. My big mouth caused me trouble by slandering people and led to legal troubles. Still, I was happy when I found a weak person who cared about what I'd have to say about them. That's when I really ran my mouth against them. Workplaces that had a lot of *my-kind* employed had real morale problems and in some places there were so many of us until *mess* became the status-quo, especially on state and federal jobs.

Weak people who didn't have enough sense *or* enough self-esteem to ignore me were my favorite sport for poking fun and setting them up to react to my hidden instigation. That's the way me and others like me would get our jollies degrading people, making people lose it, and making people feel bad about themselves and making them lose their jobs. We need to stop looking at what THEY are doing, and look at what WE are doing.

Why can't I keep a job? First of all, I don't want to work because it's too easy to live off other people. But when I do work I am so messy that I can't keep a job for long because I never learned to close my mouth. I'd never realized I caused suffering to myself because I suffered as a busybody, a murderer, and a thief, always in other folks business and leaving myself to ruin (1 Peter 4:16). I'd always try to take other folk's authority, stuff, happiness, reputation, and even their lives. Oh, yes! Lots of us are gifted and talented, but most of us never reach our potential because we spend all of our time being messy, running-down, and running other people and things that are not our charge. I caused suffering and I also suffered from opening my big mouth, but never knew why I suffered, so I just blamed the devil and other people.

And don't take me to a restaurant. Waitresses hate to see us coming because we are some of the worst folks on earth in public. We go to restaurants and talk crazy to the wait staff, are demanding and won't leave a tip. We figure all kinds of ways to get free food and services, are demanding and make scenes, embarrassing all of us. And Facebook, YouTube, and public fighting in the media makes you wonder if we are civilized at all? Everybody hates to see us coming, even ourselves. So, we need to step up! After all God has brought us through with Martin Luther King, shamefully, we are still the worst off?

Some do not find success not because they are without talent. They lack success because they have no order. One must have talent or must be teachable in order to find success. If we have talent it can be developed, but when we have no talent and no order we can't even be taught. So we continue to suffer the consequences of being out-of-order and in denial—*I am the cause of my own misery.* I continue to play the victim while I am really the victimizer. It's easier to start mess than to face myself.

So, I continue to start mess for the heck of it because I don't care about anyone or myself. Ronies make life a living hell for everyone everywhere they go. Choice? What's a choice?

REAL HELP

I didn't understand that *I* am the only one who can change my life with the help of the King. I didn't learn that *not making a choice* is still *making a choice.* I didn't learn that whether I own what I've done or not, I will still have to pay for it.

Understanding that I am being or acting like a Roni is not *all* bad when other Roni's know it too. This is only of value when I am isolated with Roni and have to defend myself from Roni because Roni-talk and Roni-act is the only language that some of us understand. Consequently, I learned that everything about Roni is not bad. Roni is helpful in some cases to help you in a helpless situation.

However, these cases are few and I can avoid them by doing a few simple things—not answering the phone, hanging up the phone, not opening the door, shutting the door, shutting my mouth, getting away from Roni, becoming emotionally and financially independent, and giving myself self-control, not someone else's control. Just because I have to act like Roni in a jam, doesn't mean I have to act like Roni now. The world understands when Roni is a desperate failure to save your life, but Roni-dom for nothing is *not* acceptable

IT'S ABOUT TIME

Eventually, I learned, *you can't help what you were born into, but you can help what you do about it.* It might take a while to unlearn what you had to become in Roniland, but you can relearn how to be civil and not lawless, cordial but firm and confident as a lion. Then my life changed for the better and I began to have a relationship with the King. This is the perception we need to have of ourselves in order and to know whose and who we are—as a lamb, as a lion, and as a dove. We are a Child of the King and we demonstrate this identity by showing, knowing, and obeying the King.

Therefore, we can always—show that we are a lamb, know that we are a lion, and go with the voice of the King.

Not being able to hear your internal voice, which is the King's voice inside of you, is the most tragic aspect of being Roni. Without your inner voice, you travel through life as a fool, unable to protect yourself, guide yourself, or know what to do to get yourself out of Roni-dom. There are many who say they are hearing God's voice, who are lying on God. I'm so glad that I learned to hear God's voice. Now I am not distracted or deceived by any other voice.

THEY'RE LYING ABOUT GOD

God doesn't say anything that He does not support in the His Word, but Ronies put God in Roni-mess. God has nothing to do with mess; therefore, God is not in our N-mess. We are only fooling ourselves believing that we can put Him in our mess. We lie about God on social media, saying what God has told us when God is not anywhere in our lies, mess, confusion, and pies in the sky mentality. We don't know who we are so we put God in stuff where He does not dwell—in darkness, in confusion, and out of order, faithlessness, rage, jealousy, envy and hatred. God is *all* love and nothing else.

Knowing who you are as a lion, lamb, and dove will allow you to always present yourself as who you really are—a child of the King. Then you will have an elevator that no one can stop from going up, especially you.

I say, "No one is any better than anyone else, but some of us are better off because we make better-choices." We can make better choices because it is within our being to do so. And it's not your being that's flawed; it's your doing, and you can change your doing by transforming yourself into whom you were meant to be—A child of the King. We can change the being through transforming oneself to the will of God and the doing will automatically change! This power of choice equalizes the odds for us. We must understand that choice is everything, no matter the path we take. It's on you! Yes, everyone has a different path with some being worse than others, but whatever path you are on can be made straight when you show the lamb, know you are a lion, and go with the voice of the King that is right inside of you to guide you. In some cases it is not an insult for some people to think you are Roni. Matter of fact, one of Roni's main flaw is to discredit others who rightly march to a different drummer, follow rules, and expect them to act right. Ronies have five main insults that identify how he/she really feels about you. These main insults are:

PRIMARY RONI INSULT	WHAT IS SAID	WHAT IS MEANT
Dislike	"There's just something about him/her/you."	I don't like you but I don't know why; so I'll just make my

		dislike about you!
Jealousy/Envy	"He/she does whatever he/she wants to do."	You won't do what he/she wants you to do when truth is, everyone does what they want to do.
Projection (Other Directed)	Saying something about the way you look: ex: You are too tall; you are too short; you are white/black; you think you are all that, etc.	I am insecure about my own appearance so I project what I am feeling on to you. When I compare myself to you I come up on the short end and make it about you.
Covetousness/Greed	"You are stingy and selfish and think of nobody but yourself."	I want you to give me your stuff because I don't want to go work for what I want; so I criticize you because you went and worked for your stuff.
Hateration/Jealousy (Slef-Hatred)	He/she thinks he's/she's white, better than me, us. You think you are all that? Who do you think you are?	Someone has good manners and the person speaking is impressed but is to hateful to give the person a compliment, rather insults them

Ronies are always giving out Roni-Insults, but don't let them bother you. They think it makes you feel bad when they call you stingy for not loaning them any money. You can't loan Roni any money because he won't pay you back. Then they say of you, "You ought to be ashamed of yourself for being stingy and not sharing with them because God is not in you." They have the nerve to try to make a potential lender feel guilty about loaning money to them that they won't pay back. They have the nerve to stop speaking to you and stick their noses up in the air against you when they owe you as if you owe them. So, you can't loan Roni no money. *If you can't give it, don't loan cause you ain't getting it back.* They think it's okay to do these things.

And Ronies call responsible black people "White-wannabes," "selfish," "ungodly," "sidity," and "crazy." But it is not an insult for Roni to think you are the C-Word or to make Roni Insults because Roni won't leave you alone unless he thinks you are crazy. Roni's first discrediting act is to call you crazy to cover-up their wrongdoing and scorn you because you won't give nothing for free. Tell them GYOSY and GYOSYN (*go get yo own stuff yoself N--*) because they think you are a Wells Fargo. A Roni is always trying to get something for nothing but you must hold your ground because if you don't you'll be just as broke and lazy as Roni is. **Speak Truth In Love!**

Dear Christian family,

Don't play me stupid!
The daddy I got wasn't orchestrated by Cupid,
The marriage and birth dates let everybody know,
He never touched my mama in time for y'alls' lie to go!
I was a bun in the oven, done before the oven ever got warm,
But you can't cover up a lie with a lie because buns get grown,
The dummy y'all picked out wasn't stupid enough,
Knowing I wasn't his kid he saw me as fair game,
Mattered not my birth certificate bore his name,
But already done buns in the oven grow up should "rape" they survive,
And fake legitimacy fails when information and demonstration don't jibe,
So whenever you give a bastard a daddy,

Please make sure he's a complete stupid-fool,
Because it ain't right to go on praising the Lord,
When you done left a baby to get screwed!
Amen Lights and Walls!

"C" Word Discrediting Game

No doubt the Discrediting Game will be used to discredit me for writing this book, because Roni and has followed my family's example to call me "crazy, " to cover-up their wrongdoing toward me with a crazy pedophile man they tried to make my daddy who said to me, "I never touched yo Mama in time for that lie." He tortured me as a result. The family knew, looked away, and blamed me. As a result of their foolery, I should be crazy, but with God's intervention on my best effort, I am not crazy. Despite the Ronidom of my early life, I have accomplished a few things to shape the world and have found independence with the King as my Savior. Roni calls you crazy to cover up his evil against you. So, it is not an insult for Roni to call you crazy; it's an insult to be called nice, because then Roni will take advantage of you and use you. Unless Roni thinks you are crazy, he's going to mess with you; so when it comes to Roni, the C-word is okay and it works for me!

Six Lessons Profitable For Surviving Roniville

Again, should you hit rock bottom, as I did and find yourself in Roniland, remember it's not an insult for Roni to think you are crazy. Roniland is real and different from the reality Non-Ronies expect and know. So if you end up there, you must know how to survive it. Again, it's not an insult for Roni to call you crazy. It's insult for Roni to call you sane, sweet, and nice because he'll run over you and use you if he thinks otherwise. So, minimally, you might need to show Roni your lion teeth, but never touch, claw them, or roar; call the police on Roni when he doesn't know what "stop" and "no" means, which happens more than not. If you try to handle them yourselves, they will get you into trouble with the police. You must know the Six Lessons in order to survive Roni and to survive Racism. You must know how to stop talking; how to stand up straight and pay attention; how to keep your eyes on who is talking considering the source, meaning you should not give credit where there is none and you must know what to say to whom or else your life will take a nose dive fooling around with Roni, be it a look-alike or a racist person. I was shocked to learn that sadly, Roni doesn't respond to normal speech, even when Roni looks like me. As a helper, I struggle with the ethical dilemma of speaking to N— in the language they can understand or leaving them to the perils of ignorance. *Ain't nobody got time for begging, broke, busted, insulting, can't be trusted Ronies!* Broke friends, broke preachers, broke family—just broke. Yet, I want to help my Ronies!

My Contradiction

Crude Talk, Teaching, and Therapy is all N— understand because that's the language they grew up with. Certainly, I don't want to lower myself to "cussing," but I also don't want to leave N— behind by speaking a language they do not understand. Maybe yelling and profanity needs to be an acceptable language for certain people. I am ashamed to say that it is effective for certain people and I have used it when all else seemed to fail. I felt bad about what using crudity to help N—, but felt good that I was able to lift them up by any means necessary.

Yea, I get a, "Shame on you," for using crudity to save my N—, but I think of what Paul said, *"To the weak I became weak, to win the weak. I have become all things to all men so that by all possible means I might save some (1 Cor 9:22; NIV)."* And then there is Pastor Iglehart's utterance to me, "Your profane is profound!"

142

I know we can't save everybody, that we should not cast pearls to swine, that we should not give holy things to unholy folks, and that we should not appear evil, but I still want everyone to have a fair chance to succeed. How can you hear the teacher use regular English when you grew up on Crude Talk? When you grow up on Crude Talk you need to hear Crude Teaching and Crude Therapy to understand what is being said. Roni is worth me lowering myself to reach him but I haven't made up my mind if I will go with crudity as a customary service to the N— public. We'll see.

N— don't know what you mean when you are not swearing, cussing, and threatening them. No wonder when their children go to school they don't know what the teacher means when they've heard all of their lives, "Shut your dog-gone-ass up and get out of my face," meaning they should not ask anything and pretend as if they don't exist because your Mama doesn't want to be bothered with you or even feed you. So the level of politeness the person has grown up with, will determine the level of low-downiness you will have to verbalize to get N— to understand what you mean. There is a difference between what N— have been conditioned to hear than what Non-N— have been conditioned to hear.

For example:

GOAL OF TALK	STANDARD TALK	CRUDE TALK
Quietness	Please be quiet/Close your mouth/Stop talking	Shut yo a..s up
Attentiveness	Please keep your eyes on the teacher/ Look at your work as you complete it	Stop being nosey/Tend to yo business

Order	Sit quietly and do not talk	Sit yo a...s down and shut yo a..s up
Doing and Finishing Work	Stay on task until you complete your work	Get yo home work, fool and stay out of my face before I kick your little a..s

I Can't Hear You

The inability to hear normal speaking due to being conditioned to hear loud and abusive speaking causes N— to suffer an Ear-To-Hear Learning Loss. Ronies are very rude and disrespectful to each other at home; so it's very hard for us to adapt and learn in a world that doesn't yell at us, threaten us, swear at us or put us down to get positive results. Many of our little girls are exposed to being called all kinds of "bitches" by our own mothers. So, if you mother calls you a "bi....," how in the world is a black woman to resist being called a bi...... by a man who is telling her he loves her while calling her a bi......? Truth is, when your mother calls you a bi...... with a slap to your face, it's nothing to accept a man calling you a bi..... with a kiss to your lips. And sadly, this kind of rearing is accepted as black culture; so Child Protective Services won't even intervene because this kind of N— training of children is seen as what black people do. But this is not black, this is N—.

I understand how hard it might be for our kids to learn when they speak another language—Crude Talk. Again, this crudity will vary from person to person but the level of crudity needed to communicate with N— will depend on the level of the crudity they are/were reared on. Some people just need a little hint and they won't bother you, but certain people need force when crudity does not work. This is when you call the police; don't use crudity or anything to try and communicate because it could cost you your life, your job or your freedom.

So, call the police on Roni when he or she doesn't know what "No" and "Stop" mean. Don't put your hands on them. When you touch trash, you will get dirty. Let the police do their job and hope they are law-abiding and will not kill Roni or you. Still, it's okay to tell! *Cause ain't nobody got time for Ronies!* And don't worry about Roni calling you a snitch because Roni is always doing something wrong and then doesn't want you to say it; when you

> IT IS OKAY TO CALL THE POLICE ON RONI WHEN NECESSARY BECAUSE TRUTH IS OPEN AND UNCOVERED. DARKNESS IS HIDDEN AND THEREFORE, EVIL.

are not lying, not scheming but only measuring and reporting what Roni has done. Measuring or knowing a fruit by what is bears is not judging; this is categorizing and you must categorize to make good decisions for yourself. So don't bother with N— talking about you because that's all they do is talk and do nothing to improve their situations.

Don't Keep a Secret With the Devil

Instead of Roni telling people not to tell, he needs to understand that he should not give people anything to tell. So tell it, tell it, and tell it to the proper authority because Roni doesn't know what is right until he is in front of a judge or a piece of steel. Roni needs to attend to his own business and stop telling other citizens who are not afraid of the police what to tell the police about them. It is OK to tell on Roni when he has wronged you but Roni wants to do you wrong and wants you to keep quiet about it. Again, it's OK to tell on Roni cause he's the devil and you can't keep a secret with him because, *you are as sick as your secret.* Keep no secrets with evil people nor with anyone because even an innocent secret becomes evil. Truth is open and uncovered. Darkness is hidden and therefore, evil.

Ronies do not even like Ronies—always crying about a snitch, always begging, always whining, always bullying, always talking noise, and always trashing the place. Ronies will give you hell on earth and then make you miss heaven in eternity. We have chopped each other up so badly until we've made the world want to chop us up; and they are doing it now. They don't understand why they can't call us the NWord with us calling each other the NWord. I don't believe in censoring free speech, but I also don't believe in personalized name-calling. But as it pertains to a character some people do meet the category of being a NWord. The world has the wrong perception of who we are from the misrepresentation of who we are from a preponderance of evidence from NWords who misrepresent Black Americans. America does not respect us as a whole. All American wants us to do is to play ball, fight in contests, perform music, tell jokes, and fight wars. So, we must let the world know that Roni is *not Black* and we must show and tell Roni, GYOSY (geeosy), *"Go get yo own stuff yoself, cause I ain't giving you nothing,"* or Roni will continue to ruin everyone's lives.

Finding the answers

Since all of us can be Ronies, remember, don't feel bad about yourself for being or acting like a Roni. All have done wrong (Romans 3:23) and all were born to do wrong (Psalms 51:5), but we *can* do the right thing when we are connected to whom we are right inside ourselves(John 15)—The King—and when we are connected with Him we can make the right choices.

My Problem

When I was trying to flee Roni-dom, I didn't know of all the help available to me. I learned to use all available resources-- good and perfect gifts, all from the Father--including medical care, social services, counseling, self-help books, support groups, AA, NA, CODA, and spiritual help, prayer and meditation, faith and a relationship with Jesus Christ. I understood that rarely have those failed who follow these paths, though following these paths does not work for those who merely need it, but only for those who want it. There is help for everyone, so that everyone is without excuse because of The King.

My Healing

I must be desensitized to hurtful words like the N-Word, the c-word (crazy), the u-word (ugly), and the s-word (stupid). If words hurt you, you will always be hurt and feel hurt. When words hurts you , the enemy will always send someone to say them to you. You are who God says you are and not who people say you are. When you learn from His word who he says you are, don't allow people to define you. Allowing people to define you will take your focus off what you need to be doing which is loving yourself, loving the King, and loving other people! Moreover, in order to heal we can make use of every good and every perfect gift because they all come from the King to heal you.

My Hearing

You must first control yourself by closing your mouth, and sitting yourself down somewhere, following directions, staying on task until completion, and keeping your hands to yourself. Keeping your hands and mouths to yourself is your best way to keep the greatest commandment—to treat others as yourself. You must demonstrate these Six Lessons. Then and only then can you begin to hear your own voice or God's voice within you. This voice will lead you onto God's path and this will make your life have meaning, purpose, success, and happiness.

LESSONS I LEARNED ABOUT LIFE

When I learned these lessons, my life began to improve. What I learned about life:

> ### To Raise My Standard of Living I learned how to:
>
> ### Love
> I must love and respect myself and others
>
> ### Focus
> I must focus on myself and not others
>
> ### Work
> I must work on a job. Work if I can work or replace money that I could have made with disability benefits if I cannot work, because it takes money to live.

Learning the Right Thing

Life is a gift, but also presents grief. We must choose what to take on and what to leave alone. We need to be able to hear our own inner voice (God's voice) to do this. Oftentimes, bad things happen to good people, and we have trouble hearing this voice. When this happens, The King has our backs and gives us an elevator. But even a King-given elevator won't work if we shoot ourselves in our feet. All we must to do our best to choose the right thing and God will bring about the rest!

What and Whom We Listen To

A major source poisoning to our minds is the TV, a one-eyed devil that teaches us to do whatever we want to do. But we must turn this idea of "anything goes" around and be the best we can be (even if our best sucks to other people). God knows when we are doing our best and it doesn't matter what anybody else thinks as long as you are not causing them to think badly of you. Sadly, TV often makes us feel proud of being silly, messy, lazy, nasty, overweight, bad-acting, drug-doing, acting a fool, and disregarding family values, as if life has no standards. By having no standard, we have made our consciences so hard that we feel no guilt or shame for our wrongdoing. When we are wrong, guilt and shame are there to let us know God is not pleased and we need to correct our behavior. God will help us when we have the will to do what is right. We must pray, "Father, create in me some act-right and renew a right-desire in me." So, you see, we had some act-right and a right-desire, but lost it with help from those who we see being in charge, but we have more help from God to get our act-right back.

We Need Order

Society now teaches us that whatever I feel and whatever I do is right, and that nobody and nothing matters. Parents try to tell the teachers how to do their jobs, when they have not been trained to teach anything and can't even raise their own children. So, what gives them the gall to think they can teach the teacher? Our bad-acting and wrongly protective parents are causing us to fail and they act like they can't hear the world saying, "We don't care about what your problem is; you've got to act right or we will dispose of you." Some parents do nothing to help us to be successful as adults in a world that requires good manners, excellence, and skill. They teach their children that is not important to say, "Please," "Thank you," "Yes, ma'am," "Yes, sir," and "No, sir." These foolish-acting parents think this makes us act like slaves when they are not teaching their children how to placate people. If nothing more than to keep them from harming and injuring us and failure to teach kids to be courteous causes a missed opportunity about knowing behavior that will bring favor. "Yes, ma'am" and "No, ma'am," "Please" and "Thank you" have landed many opportunities, but many miss out. Our rebellion and disrespect are destroying us. We can correct this if we'd listen and learn to do things the right way. Any and everything does not go!

Before Roni-parents took over the schools, rational parents

understood their children were God's children and they put their children in the hands of Godly people who did what was best. I know there are some rotten apples in every bunch, but rotten parents destroyed the good apples and left us most of the rotten ones. When rational-parents respected the teachers, it didn't matter if they liked how Godly people did what they did to discipline their children, as long as they did not abuse them. They knew their children needed to learn to obey all adults in authority, because they weren't going to be with their children all of their lives.

Nowadays, Roni parents don't want anyone to chastise their children, and they side with their children against adults when the children are wrong. So, parents end up protecting bad-acting children in their wrongdoing. This only sets their children up for failure, abuse, and to be destroyed because they have spoiled their children and made them unable to cope and succeed in life. It's almost better to be abused than to be spoiled; at least abused people get an elevator, whereas spoiled children are left to their own destruction and get no elevator. Dumb-acting parents spoil their children by sparing the rod. However, the proper use of the rod to discipline is not an option for angry and foolish parents. Truth is, using the rod of correction in a non-abusive way is what some children need or else they will be totally lost. Too bad, many parents won't take the time or have the patience to not retaliate against their children in the best interest of the child and use spanking appropriately.

A book I am writing titled, *Mr. Wiggly Spanks*, offers an appropriate way to use the rod to help bad-acting children by using non-abusive spanking that will not result in spoiling or injuring them. Maybe Mr. Wiggly will tell a story about himself, too, like I am telling about myself, Roni, to help parents get some act-right from their children. Parents need help, too.

Everything I'd learned was mostly wrong. I had to unlearn wrong stuff and relearn the right stuff. It was hard to teach myself what was right because at first, I thought whatever I felt was right, but I realized that I can't go by my feelings, but should go with what I know and just because I feel a certain kind of way, doesn't mean I'm right. Truly, what often feels right is not right; so we have to go back and refocus our attention on what we know instead of what we feel. Good thing if we don't know what is right we have God's word to teach us and a conscience to alert us to what is right. When I decided to unlearn and relearn, the King, was right there to help me to change for the better.

LESSONS I RELEARNED ABOUT LIFE—HOW I UPDATED MY FAULTY LEARNING

If we want society to know that Black Lives Matter, we must collectively show that virtue matters. We are not showing this because of our disproportionate numbers of bad-actors who misrepresent Black lives and Black lives will never matter within the context of the misrepresentation of black citizens by blacks in charge and by blacks in the public eye. Our lives will matter when virtue matters among us as a whole. Right now the few are suffering for the whole because we have given the impression that all of us are NWords but everything black is not a Nword and need not suffer but we need to start to look better by acting better if we want to start to get better treatment and make our lives matter. Here are some of the qualities things that must matter if we matter:

1. THE KING MATTERS: When we understand that we didn't create ourselves but were created from a source greater than what we can see, we can learn to have a love and respect for the King, ourselves, and others. We won't matter as long as God doesn't matter. Not church, I said God—righteousness, peace, truth, love, holiness.

2. MANNERS DO MATTER: We cannot be a good person if we are a bad citizen. And who doesn't know, don't chew (gum or food) in a formal setting? Who doesn't know to keep your conversations private and that no one wants to hear your conversation, profanity, or come-ons? Ronies don't know these things! Good Etiquette is not a White thing; it is a good citizen thing. We must become good citizens before we can become a good Christian. We won't matter as long as good manners don't matter.

3. MONEY: HAVING YOUR OWN MONEY DOES MATTER: If you have no money, you cannot eat and if you cannot eat, you will steal and if you steal, you will kill, too. So, we need our own money and there are two good choices:

1: Work income for those who can work.

2. Disability income for those who cannot work. Society must take care of those who cannot work and these persons should not be scorned or blamed for their inability. But people who can work need to go to work. Roni discredits the need to have his or her own personal money because he or she feels completely comfortable begging and tricking other people out of their money. Roni does know that everybody else is saying to him or her, "If you don't want any money and are happy with Jesus alone, then stay that way, but just don't ask me (taxpayers) for my money because I am not and don't want to give Roni anything. And get your money the right way by working for it because money gotten wrong won't last long!" We won't begin to matter as long as having your own money doesn't matter.

4. MORALS (RIGHT AND WRONG) MATTER: You can't make right become wrong and wrong become right. If you do, you won't know right from wrong or how to correct your behavior so you won't suffer for your wrongs. We will not matter as long as morals don't matter.

5. RULES MATTER: There is a way to do everything that we do and those are rules. Most rules are known inside of us-- conscience--but these same rules are taught in schools, in the Bible, and should be taught in our homes. When we follow rules, we stand the best chance of being successful. We won't matter as long as rules don't matter.

6. EDUCATION MATTERS: Getting a good education, not a nothing education or degree, for most of us, is our only way out of poverty, because the TV is not going to make every Roni a star-player, all of us are not going to be NBA stars, and everybody is not going to get rich from marketing plans.

We let the TV trick us into believing we don't need to obey the law or go to school to get a quality education. And I'm not talking about getting degrees and letters behind our names, but about getting knowledge with those degrees letters because we know too many of us slip and slide through school and get the paper but have no knowledge; I'm talking about getting knowledge not getting letters and papers. Getting educated is a challenge right now, because schooling is too tainted by the love of money and not the love of students. So students must take charge of making sure they are getting a good education and teach themselves. In other words: Don't look for help because it's up to you. Help yourself! We can help ourselves through proficiently and thoroughly reading every subject area—English, Math, Social Science, Physical Science, Music and Arts, and by learning hands on trades and skills. You should know what jobs are trending and are upcoming for the future and you can get information from the Department of Labor and Employment Commission.

We need to value and pursue knowledge in the course of being educated, especially before having babies that we cannot afford to take care of and we need to stop committing felonies that keep us from becoming successful. We need to stop doing what we feel and do what we don't want to do--act right and get a good education. Public schools systems are not places where students can expect to get a good education because these systems serve a duplicitous purpose, i.e., either as a College Bound Launch or a Cooling Board Lynch. It's up to the student which experience he or she will make of their public schooling.

So, it's up to you to decide if you will gain knowledge or if you will pass through the so-called educational system wasting everybody's and your own time. If you don't want to benefit from the books and study helps available in the system it will be your Cooling Board Lynch that buries your success. But if you do want to benefit from the books and study helps available in the system you will take these tools and first be your own and first teacher and teach yourself and then let the teachers who care about teaching help you to learn; this way the educational system will be a College Bound Launch for you, giving you a launching pad into success. The choice of getting a good education is up to you but you alone must decide if getting a good education matters to you! Now hear this! The school system is where white folks benefit from the making of Roni by Black folks. Roni makes us then White-folks can break us because Roni has put us at a disadvantage making us unable to function or compete in the world of true knowledge and excellence, primarily because we want to keep up mess, act a fool, do nothing, and get something for nothing at school and at work.

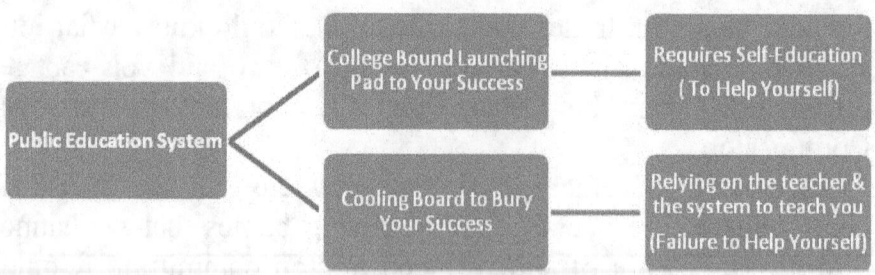

Lessons I Relearned (Quick Look)

- The King Matters
- Good Manners Do Matter
- Having Your Own Money Matters
- Morals Matter
- Rules Matters
- Education Matters
- Modesty Matters
- Being the Leader Matters
- What I Do with My Money Matters
- I Matter

How can you know your rights, if you can't read what they are? Again, even with all of this chaos going on, you can gain knowledge and the paper that shows you've gained knowledge if you will take the helm of your learning ship and do what Big Mama told me to do, *"Don't worry about what everybody else is doing; just tend to your own business, don't worry about the teacher not helping you. Help yourself and read those old handed down from the White-school book and know everything in them! And don't worry about people not liking you and about them mistreating you, just love yourself and love your enemies and read everything good you can, and do what's right and listen to God and God will bless you!"*

We can either take the launch or take the lynching, but the choice is ours because getting a good education does matter. We won't matter as long as getting a good education does not matter.

7. MODESTY MATTERS: Since life is not a club or a beach, we Ronies need to learn to dress in modest clothing for day-time wear. Women show so much skin until a man doesn't have to imagine what's under our skirt. Roni men show their butt-cracks until they gross-out everybody, making them think of the only place a butt should be open to--the toilet. Nobody wants to be reminded of a toilet! This lack of modesty and decency causes us to cheapen our bodies and gives the wrong signal; Yet, "No" means "No" and no matter how we dress no one has the right to touch us in the wrong way. But we do need modesty. I don't know what makes young Roni girls and boys want to display themselves to look like thugs, prostitutes, and whores. I don't know why we go to a church looking like we're going to a club. I don't know why we walk around in house and beach clothing in public. I don't know why we don't know how to act or how to dress. We don't understand that modesty does matter. We can give a possible admirer no room to imagine because we show everything we've got. But modesty does matter. To this, Big Mama used to say, "If you ain't for sale, take down your sign." Since modesty does matter, we need to put on some clothes when we are on the street because life is not a beach, bathroom, or a nightclub. We won't matter as long as being modest does not matter.

8. RESPECTING AUTHORITY MATTERS: Ronies primary problem is the disrespect for authority. This causes him to: 1. be insubordinate (rebellious) and 2. to be nosy (in other folks business). Both are because he doesn't know that authority matters. Roni needs to learn three rules: 1. Everybody must obey somebody (when you never learned to obey your parents then you're not going to know how to obey your boss; so when you get old you've got to parent yourself and teach yourself how to obey by obeying somebody else). 2. Don't run what you ain't in charge of; 3. Keep your eyes on your own paper (meaning you are to think with your own head and not expect anyone to think with your head); 4. Keep your mouth on your own plate (eat what you like the way you want and don't try to eat out of anybody else's plate, make them eat what you want, or tell them what to eat. 5. Keep your nose out of other folks business (control yourself, not other people because you are a 24/7 job, OK?). The Bible says, "But let none of you suffer as a murderer, or *as* a thief, or *as* an evildoer, or as a busybody in other men's matters (1 Peter 4:15)." We are suffering as murderers, thieves, and evildoers because we do not respect the authority of others by attending to our own authority to show that our lives do matter. We will not ever matter as long as we are in everybody else's matters and not attending to our own matters.

9. BEING THE LEADER MATTERS: Ronies have been convinced that their so-called *pastors* are not expected to live according to the Good Book because they're *just a man* or *only human.* Malarkey! Let *just a man* or *just a human* do heart surgery on you. Let *just-a-man* do brain surgery on you. Sadly, we have been completely convinced by Roni-preachers that they should not be held accountable for their behavior. But how can they lead where they do not go, and how can they teach what they do not know?

The only place these ignorant Ronies can be important is in the church where they can put on a suit and be listened to by church slaves. This is why the earth trembles--when we try to make slaves into kings, when they can't be anything but slaves and slave-makers, because you can't make a slave a king or put them in charge. They must be made free first--free of lies, free of excuses, free of laziness, and free of uncaring. Our minds stopped growing by listening to the Roni-preachers who bring nothing new to the table. They give us hash and no revelation and problem is information does not bring about transformation and certainly not lack of information. We don't expect to be taught anything new; we already know what they are going to say.

The main reason Roni-preachers can't help us is because they are slaves too. They don't have their own money and stuff.

They depend on us. So they have to say what the congregation wants them to say. If they don't the congregation won't give them money. We know they need our money; so we just do them any-kind-of-way to get our way and they don't have a choice, but to say and do what we want them to do to make us feel good about our bad acting and make us feel good like jungle bunnies, so we can run wild and do what we want to or we will cut their money off. Still they become tyrants against us, although they need because we want to be slaves as well.

FEEDING OR FLEECING?

It is very sad. Party animals with low self-esteem led by paid verbiage Nword preachers. We don't know that life is not all about feeling good, or doing what you feel. Fact is, much of life is hard, hurtful, and especially the hurtful truth, but knowing the truth will heal us. We cannot benefit from the truth always wanting to feel good, have a party, have a good time, never making allowances for feeling bad or working hard. *"Life is not a flowery bed of ease!"* But we are so suggestible until we are led into all types of deception by the egotistical and narcissistic preachers whom we allow to lead us. There is nothing sacred about the sacred desk (pulpit) these preachers stand behind. We are so desperate for love and acceptance and are irresponsible about our own lives and souls until we allow these so-call men of God to badger us in God's name and to use the pulpit as a whipping post, while taking our money.

And we say and do nothing because they've appeased our guilt and made us afraid to hold them accountable by preaching to us out of context, "Touch not God's anointed." Don't they know followers are anointed as well and they are not to touch us? Problem is with us is that we allow ourselves to forget about the truth opting to have a good time. Having a good time is good only when it compels us to be responsible because a good feeling only last for the moment but taking responsible action that takes time, is the only way positive change can occur that will last.

We are in a vicious cycle of no productivity because our preachers can't teach what they don't know and can't lead where they themselves don't go. So they give us Paid Verbiage that allows us to control each other but never grow. We are dependent on our preachers to make us feel good in our wrongdoing and to tell us what we want to hear and our preachers are dependent upon us to pay them to make us feel good and tell us what we want to hear. But... *You can't feed me when you need me neither fleece me when you teach me!*

Roni preachers are nothing more than pimps and playboys who seduce, manipulate, and depend on the women to take care of them. They string all the women along in secret-silence making them all feel that they are "the one," so they can control them and keep their allegiance to do things for them that a wife would do, even if they have a wife, who if there is a wife, she is ignored and disrespected because he knows if he doesn't woo the women they won't take care of him, pay tithes, give offerings and give him extra money to live on.

Church Harem?

The preacher's harem, called a church, is the only place the Roni-preacher can have nothing and be nothing and still get treated as if he is godly, respectable, and intelligent. He can have no education, no training, no order, and no anointing, work on a dump truck and put on a suit on Sunday morning, get up in the pulpit and dumb Ronies will let him boss them around in God's name depending on how much personal charisma and sex appeal he has. The church is the only place where desperate women will accept any remnant of appreciation and love and stringing-along just to be able to feel that they are special. Truth is, none of these women are special, but are only being used by a sorry man called a preacher/pastor, because he doesn't have his own stuff. These men string some women along by giving them marriage proposals that never materialize, and they string others along with flattery, butt-rubs, palm-tickles, sexual come-ons, nocturnal sexual assaults, and with neediness. In actuality, they are not anybody any woman would want because they have nothing—no money, no home, no health insurance—and would be nothing but a financial and health burden to a wife. But some women are so stupid and desperate to be a preacher's wife until they will take in any britches and breath in the pulpit.

These men play the "candy-man" who lures weak and sick women into their traps isolating one victim who protects him from touching the others and they use a woman's cry for help as an opportunity to help themselves to the woman. These so-called preachers and deacons are nothing but dogs that molest the child in women and disrespect the woman they are because they abuse their authority to exploit, control, and abuse women all in God's name. They are good at keeping a woman in secret so that they can use her for various reasons; some of the secretly kept women are aware of their secret place and some are not because he will keep his target woman a secret as long as he can so that the other pups won't know that he has made a pick of the litter and stop serving him. Even when these men have been trained in accredited colleges they do not transfer their knowledge to the pews because they want to keep us enslaved to being used and deceived. And white folks have nothing to do with this. Our so-called preachers and Bible teachers who have knowledge leave their knowledge in the field to rot as does a poacher who leaves his game to rot in the field and does not benefit from roasting it. The Bible calls such men lazy and ungodly (Proverbs 12:27) but yet we follow them. We are enslaved by our own NWord preachers who teach us a NWord Theology.

Preacher or Poacher?

I never understood the detriment of an incompetent preacher until I observed a seminary trained so-called pastor use his position to lord over, control, manipulate, and abuse the people; dethrone God with himself, and make slaves of the people for himself and he didn't even have his own money. He was abusing the people while using them, especially the women. Unbelievable? This feigned leader set the profile for a premier N- preacher who did nothing but acted a fool in the pulpit and talked in esoteric riddles that helped no one. But surprisingly, the followers seemed to like being dogged, and they liked being slaves; because they didn't want to be accountable as well. He lived in the church parsonage, didn't have his own money, and was dependent on the members for his livelihood. How can you lead people whom you are dependent upon? You can't! And how can you lead people when you cannot afford to speak truth to them? You can't! You must compromise yourself and the truth when you don't have enough to take care for yourself on your own and this is what this poacher did.

Sadly, we cannot learn anything because our preachers are so needy and greedy until they refuse to teach us in the way we should go. So, even education doesn't help us because we won't teach the truth that we know and this is what Dr. Paterson, president of Southwestern Seminary, referred to as poaching and not preaching (Spring Graduation 2015). These poaching preachers fail to teach us what they know because they are dependent upon the pews financially. They ain't got no money! Not their own money, only have what the people give them because they don't want to work as well. So they have to compromise what they teach and give the people a "feel good" "no standards" fake gospel message. Sadly, too often an educated pew allows themselves to be subjected to an ignorant pulpit, causing the blind to lead the blind right into a lake of despair, disease, death, prison, destruction, poverty, and eventually the lake of fire. Thus we have the Dualism of Black-on-Black Ignorance, which is that those who know will not teach and those who do not know cannot teach. Who will help us to learn and grow? Roni preachers cannot help us to learn or grow; they will only do so if we close our purses and require they lead because being the leader does matter.

SEGREGATION VS. INTEGRATION
The Segregation Advantage

Roni and Roni-preachers cry about the worst thing to happen to us was integration claiming we adopted ways that went against doing right when we integrated, and the White people took the prayer, the paddle and putting-out of bad-actors out of the schools too with that integration and now we have weapons, guns, truancy, violence, bullying, and no learning going on at the schools and we are just filling up the jails. Also, integration tricked us by telling us we are equal and by telling us we have rights, when before integration we knew we weren't equal and knew we had to do three to four times better and work three to four times harder. We were the last hired, first fired, had to be better than (excel beyond) the rest, and would get the maximum penalty in the Whiteman's court. Truth is, we still are not equal and do not have rights, but we've been tricked into thinking we have rights and are equal.

The I.D. (Integration Disadvantage)

We think the Integration Disadvantage was learning things like letting children speak their minds and do what they want to do from the White folks, *but that ain't it*; it was really forgetting the eight truths we know about America and *us's* which are:
(1) We are not equal and must live with a unequal-double standard; ex: When we are sick we are being lazy and when they are sick they are really sick; when we can't do the job

we are fired and when they can't do the job they are retired
(2) We will be the last hired and first fired
(3) We have to be three to four times better to achieve less or the same
(4) We must do the right thing and God will be on our side
(5) We won't get fair treatment
(6) When we do wrong we will get the max penalty; *so don't expect justice or mercy nor any money from yo Mama or Daddy cause if you went to jail you were on your own cause you didn't have to choose to go to jail,*
(7) The law is designed to hurt us not to help us. It is still consistent with what the White policeman told me over 40 years ago when I went to them for help because my birth parents were abusing me indicating to me that, "The law wasn't and isn't made to help us and that the law opines that we deserve injustice." Thus, there is no justice for us; therefore our only hope is in Jesus and this requires us to follow His ways, not follow or emulate bad actors, at church, in the community, home, school, or on the TV.
(8) The world hates those who love and are loved by God, but the world cannot destroy us because God gives favor to anyone who submits to Him and to those who are forsaken. This doesn't mean we won't be injured or killed. Nonetheless, our spiritual man will not be destroyed. However, because we do not honor God we receive the wrath of man and the wrath of God; so we must live right and our favor will not be hindered, because when God is for us no one else who is against us matters. Yes! We need God's favor
(9) Anyone can receive God's grace and mercy when we are little in our own eyes and recognize our need for God. This need for God must be demonstrated by our obedience to God. When we know these facts we will be empowered to overcome the trap of Roni-dom that leads us to a substandard

level of life that keeps us enslaved to ignorance, disrespect, incarceration, disease, and poverty. Teaching these facts will give us the ability to discern how to survive American racism, and help us overcome the integration disadvantage!

(10) We must obey the law to avoid the injustice of the law. When we obey the law we are in the best position to make the law work for us because Caesar must enforce what it decrees even for us.

We *ain't* equal and we've got to be BETTER! Sadly, we are not considered equal in the real world although the Constitution says that we are. Thus, we must understand that we must do more and gain more to get the same or better. And most of all we cannot act like everyone else; we will get the maximum disadvantage when we are wrong. So, we've got to be better than (excel beyond) the rest; this is what my generation was taught and is what I taught my black sons. In other words we must be more prepared, better mannered, better educated, and more skilled. We must understand this and know that we cannot put our guards down to think we are equal to white folks. We can see how white folks are doing President Obama. This lets us know we aren't equal, no matter how many laws have been passed, because we cannot legislate love or respect. Hatred against our first black President shows us that America will always see us as a nigger. So, loving and respecting ourselves and others is our only choice and this is a choice that only we can make. When we decide we are going to love and respect ourselves and others regardless of what someone else does we will become a people of integrity who know the truth about the way the world operates. Then we will regain the resilience of slavery, now lost among us.

We are last in the world right while we have some of the best talent, skill, and know how among us. God has given us an elevator so that we can come up to the starting line and take on first place; He said, "the first will be last and the last will be first." We have shot ourselves in the feet and can't even get on God's elevator that we really need because we suffer because we are not treated as equals to white folks. We are not equal to white people but we have been tricked by integration. Now we don't do anything to be better than the rest by learning and working more than the others or by learning how take being offended.

Learning to "close your mouth" is the best defense against reacting to insults, racial slurs, and abuse. Older folks knew they had to take it to make it. They were not quick to speak and slow to think. The power to excel is directly related to our ability to take crap off of white folks. No one is better than anyone else is, but when we say we must be better we mean:

- You must work harder and achieve over and above what's needed!
- You must shut your mouth and not wear your feelings on your sleeves (not openly show your feelings) and take stuff!
- Because if you don't take it, you won't make it.

We must learn how to "take stuff," because white folks will always find some way to let us know that they think we are less than—attitudes of white supremacy permeate America—and we cannot react to it if we want to get ahead and keep a level head. We've got to take some sh..t to make it; so we have to choose our battles because some stuff ain't worth it. For example, I was invited to attend a dinner with a chaplaincy class wherein I was the only black person and a white woman in the class said to me when I entered the room, "We were waiting for you to come before we ordered our drinks; how would you like some Kool-Aid? Kool-Aid? Really? Now Kool-Aid is a sugary drink made of a substance that can dye your clothing, sold in soul-food restaurants; certainly I would not be able to order Kool-Aid in a Chinese restaurant. I immediately knew this woman was making a racial slur, because in the minds of white folks we are inferior and associated with poor diet. This was offensive, but I didn't react in a defense manner. I responded, 'I'm a tea drinker," and excused myself from the dinner. An integrated habitation with segregated hearts is not true integration; thus integration is a farce. We've been tricked by the lies about integration. Integration did hurt us because we forget the truth and started believing we have rights *when we ain't got no rights and started believing that anything goes/have it your way*; we've always had to earn what we got and had a strong belief system in living right but we have seemingly forgotten this by mixing in with everybody else.

You see, we believe in spanking and we believe in correcting you where you act up. If you acted up in public, you got it in public. You go girl, Toya Graham! That's the way we did it and that's what we need to go back to; because the law will kill our children for what they won't allow us to do to raise them. We believe in spanking when it is the only way to keep the child from ruin; and we need to find a way to keep the state from not allowing us to raise our children like the Bible says, not sparing the rod when needed. Because of what was going on in Baltimore Graham's public corporal punishment was okay, but otherwise the authorities punish parents for using physical punishment.

We believe in spanking and we believe in living right because you reap what you sow; and we believe in respecting our elders because we were always taught this. We knew it took a village to raise a child, so any grown-folks in the neighborhood could chastise us for acting bad. Now, we don't want anyone correcting our children even when they are dead wrong; we don't want anyone to say anything to our children; and our children are going to hell in a hand basket and we can't do anything with them. Integration did hurt us because we adapted to White folks ways instead of sticking with our ways.

166

We started letting truth change, making excuses for bad acting, and taking up for our children when they acted bad instead of letting the village help us to raise them. We started going broke on jailbirds when we used to tell them and show them we would not spend one penny on them going to jail because they didn't have to choose to go to jail. And we have Black writers, educators, and leaders who have the nerve to blame the high numbers of Blacks in jail on the injustice of the system in catching more of the Black bad-actors than in catching the White bad-actors cause they got more police in the Black neighborhoods and that White folks can pay for lawyers to get their kids off, when they need to be telling us to "stop the crime" and your name won't even come up in the jail system. Yes, integration did hurt us, but we are to blame for this because we forgot what we know about what raises us--salvation--and about what lowers us--sin. The only way for US to get our rights is to do what's right then the King makes it right by taking us up.

We can equalize the odds against us. Our equalization plan is in the hands of the King and it is freely given to everyone who follows Him. We have always had a remedy to America's cast system against us and that is righteousness and everyone who lives Godly has this equalization plan to individually overthrow America's racism against us. We can't blame integration for what is going on right now because we have a remedy against inequality, against being oppressed, and against being deemed the least of all and that is doing right and being two to three times better.

> THE ONLY WAY FOR US TO GET OUR RIGHTS IS TO DO WHAT'S RIGHT THEN THE KING MAKES IT RIGHT BY TAKING US UP.

We also have another remedy to help us to go against the lies of integration and this is to take advantage of the **Segregation Advantage**—to awaken our own people to God because we are our own audience. Because the most segregated place in the world is the church with Ronies in charge, this presents the best opportunity for *us's* to help *us's*. Why don't Roni-preachers take advantage of the **Segregation Advantage** to offset the deleterious effects of integration? Instead, they do the same bad things to us that integration did when they know we wasn't raised like that. We are sitting with Roni-preachers every Sunday, but there is no impact on Roni for the good because Roni-preachers are doing the same thing they say integration did against us-- Asserting that we are equal and have rights, teaching us there are no standards, to do what you feel, and that we are helpless over sin, Satan, society, the self, someone else, and the system.

Real leaders will take advantage of the **Segregation Advantage** and teach our people about the reality of the illusion of American democracy; they will teach us to stop making excuses, to attend to oneself, to put in the work, and to love God and our neighbor instead of helping Roni to be tricked by deceptive political propaganda, to make excuses, to shame the King, and to blame the devil and people for what we are doing to hurt ourselves. Church-Ronies tried to get me to blame the devil for my trouble when the King's Voice taught me that people submit to the devil and choose to do bad things to other people.

Church-Ronies makes excuses for the wrong they do by saying, "The devil is busy," when fact is "The devil is invited," in their lives *'cause Satan doesn't go anywhere he's not welcomed* and will leave you if you reject him. They need to stop blaming the devil when they love darkness and go with it. Bad thing is they want to go with the darkness but don't want to pay the consequences of it so they drag you into it, but they need to have their own experience and leave other people out of their mess. People that loved told me, "Go on and have your own experience (the hard way), but I'm not going to be a part of it," so I learned to take responsibility for my problems and stop making excuses or blaming anything or anyone else.

It was not the situation that caused my problem, but my perception of the situation that caused a problem for me; if I saw the situation as the problem then it was a problem for me, but if I saw the situation as a platform for God to work a miracle then all I had to do was to wait on God and attend to my own business to put in the work I needed to do to get ahead. And even if someone is to blame for our problems, it may not be our fault, but it is still our problem that we must get help with to fix because forgiving people and looking ahead is the only way we can release the damage and move forward; so stopping at blaming isn't helpful, but taking on our problems is helpful.

In Professional Counseling and Psychotherapy we see growth in Roni and everybody else because we don't allow excuses, looking around and looking back, or failure to put in the work to get what you want. Why don't we see this same growth in the church? We see no growth due to poor and a lack of leadership. Roni-preachers don't know that leadership means walking ahead of the people, not behind them, and not with them. I don't see any leading going on among Roni-preachers and we can't blame white folks for what is going on with us when we have access to our people every Sunday. What are we doing to take advantage of this segregated time? Nothing! So rather than not holding leaders to a higher standard to demonstrate the Word and making excuses for bad leadership, we must hold our leaders accountable because good leadership does matter. Moreover, we will not matter as long as we do not matter to our own church leaders, community leaders, and television icons, who exploit, mislead, control, misrepresent us, failing to teach, failing to awaken us to truth, keeping us in a state in life where our lives do not matter to society but matter only to God because we look like a threat to society. In other words, we won't matter to others as long as we don't matter to ourselves.

If we don't matter to ourselves how can we matter to anyone else?

If your life matters, don't misrepresent yourself or the King!

Moreover, If you don't SHOW you ain't nothing, how is anybody else going KNOW you ain't nothing!

Where I put my money does matter

Roni-makers teach us to give and God will bless you even if you give to a bad cause or a bottomless pit. This is foolish because the Good Book says we reap what we sow; so, if we sow into nothing we cannot expect to receive anything other than nothing. And this is why *we ain't got nothing*; we give to nothing and let nothing people convince us that we are giving to a good cause and the only cause is to their greedy and needy pockets. Ronies don't know that he or she should not take part in the wrongdoing of others by giving them money to support their wrongdoing. But they listen to wrongdoers and let them convince themselves to give to them even though they are not examples of their own teaching and even though none of their predictions come true, like we are a bunch of stupid church fools when we are not. But where Roni gives money does matter, because it's bad to think you are building the King's Kingdom when you are building Roni-dom. So, where I give my money does matter. We won't matter as long as we put our money in a bottomless pit.

I do matter

I am Roni because I think I am a bastard to the King. But, just because I may be a bastard to the world because my daddy is absent in my life, it does not mean I am a bastard to the King. If I know I am a Child of the King, I would know that I am loved and then I could learn to love myself. I don't love myself because I have been shamed into thinking I don't deserve to be loved. And

170

I act so badly until no one wants to love me. If I know that I am a Child of the King, I'd know that I am loved, I am important, and I am good. I would know the difference between loving myself and others, and worshipping myself and others. I don't know the difference between these two things; so I worship myself and others, then I lose respect for the King.

I must love myself, but not worship myself. Worship belongs to the King and not to mortals or to things. Love is one thing and worship is another. Our problem is that we worship people and use people and love things when we should worship God, love people, and use money and things to love and express our love and worship--God's worth to us. So I should love myself, but not worship myself or anyone else, even when they teach me to worship them, instead of the King.

I learned to love myself by seeing myself through God's eyes. God doesn't see my flaws but sees past them because He knows my heart. He knows my needs and doesn't charge me with what I cannot help. I have a relationship with Him and my relationship with God helps me to love myself. He dwells with

JUST BECAUSE YOU FEEL LIKE A ZERO, DOESN'T MEAN YOU HAVE TO ACT LIKE A ZERO, OR LIVE LIKE A ZERO.

us to give us hope and direction to improve our lives. I took this hope and truth came with it; so I was led into the way of truth— which made me free to become all I can be. I became open to The Voice which leads me to salvation, safety, and success.

Passing the test of my love for myself and the King occurs when I treat others like I should treat myself. When I treat others like I should not treat myself then I know I do not love myself, since I treat others like I treat and think of myself. When I love myself I can love others and the King. When I love myself I won't put myself in harm's way or give anyone a just cause to hurt me. Loving myself is the only way for me to avoid acting like Roni. When I can show that I love myself by the way I treat myself and others, then I can learn other lessons to lead me out of Roni-dom. After all, we are to build up the Kingdom and not build up Roni-dom. So, I do matter.

When learning about me, I had to unlearn what I learned about life, what I learned about myself, and what I learned about the King because I had learned things the wrong way. We won't matter collectively as long as we do not matter individually.

Big Question: If I do not matter to myself, how can I matter to anyone else?

The self-zeroed-out effect: (Believing the lie about you).

Life comes to us in many ways and for the unfortunate we do not learn our value. Many of us don't know God's love through loving parents, family, or friends, certainly not the world; so we don't value who we are and oftentimes devalue ourselves; then comes the codependence, indifference, and abusive lifestyles wherein we are zeroed-out. But what has really happened is that we BELIEVED the lies of those faulty learning systems and then the negative impression of ourselves became self-inflicted, not necessarily in awareness, but it's something we have done to ourselves. This was my problem. I zeroed myself out by believing the negative things my abusers, haters, and oppressors said about me. When I realized this, I fixed it by changing what I believed. First I started acting like I was valuable then the good feelings were the last to show up. I did pretty good with my "zero" and so can you. Just because you feel like a zero, doesn't mean you have to act like a zero, or live like a zero.

So what we must do it to ACT better until we can GET better. This is why God just gives us instructions on how to act because He knows it's too much to understand the why's; but we can perform the act. Ex: You are not being asked to explain or agree, but to close your mouth. You are not being asked to

172

explain why you are not sitting down but to just put your bottom and your back to the back and the bottom of the seat, etc. Problem is we act-bad after already feeling bad about ourselves, adding insult to our own injury and don't know why we don't matter. First of all, you won't matter to anyone else when you are a zero to yourself. It is evident that as a group we do not love or respect ourselves and have self-inflicted a zero-self-worth. If not we would not demonstrate the kinds of shameful, immoral, uncaring, and terrorizing behavior to the word that has caused us to look like our lives do not matter. And we must first understand that this was a self-inflicted ZERO because it's all about what we believe about who we are! If you don't matter to yourself, how are you going to matter to me? **For a tree is known by its fruit (Matt 12: 33b).** You show what you know and you do what your heart holds. So who are we really? **For the mouth speaks what the heart is full of (Matt. 12:34).**

Knowing I matter,
Shows up in the way that I walk,
Knowing I matter,
Shows up in the way that I talk,
I want the world to know it,
So, I am sure to show it,
I know what it means,
To be a child of the King,
I do what is right, no matter who is wrong,
I obey my parents, at school, at play, and at home,
I'm a King's Kid,
Nothing is too good for me,
I'm a specialty,
I'm a King's kid, I'm a King's,
Oh, yes, I'm a child of the King,
That's who I act like, and it can be seen,
Oh, yes! Yes, I'm a child of the King!

LESSONS I RELEARNED ABOUT THE KING

First and foremost, I needed to understand that the King did not orchestrate or will the bad things in my life to make me better, like the church tried to tell me. That only maddened me. The King did want it to happen, didn't make it happen, but would turn it around for me when I followed his example. This allowed me to forgive what I thought God had done me wrong about and then I felt valuable knowing God's love for me and could love myself.

After I began to love myself then I could love the King. I understood that I am working for the King to shape the world into a better place and be one with the King in life and eternity. The King is in control of all things, but does not make us do anything. We have free will to act the way we want to act, even if we choose to act wrongly. The King does not make or want bad things to happen. That's why when we worship Him, he makes good of the bad.

When I met the King, from inside my heart, He taught me to lean only on Him and myself, alone. This way I won't make kings of mortals who are frail, faulty, and failing. I developed a friendship with the King and talked and listened to Him. He taught me how to live and how to get myself out of Roni-dom. I learned to lean and depend on the King, alone. Now, I am not dependent on anyone in particular. I'm so glad the King taught me this because Ronies will treat you any-kind-of-way when you are dependent upon them. Although people need people, we do not need anyone in particular. So, I do not get stuck on any one person, because the King replaces people and gives us whom we need when we need them.

And most of all, the King, makes everyone know how to act, even if no one has taught us. We all know right from wrong and we alone are accountable for our actions. We can let bad-acting parents, the fake-church, the TV, and a bad-acting State trick us into thinking it's not our own fault, but we are the ones who have to pay for what we do. The King has put the knowledge of what is right in every one of us and we can do right if we want to no matter if you have a parent/teacher or not because *the grace of God that brings salvation has appeared to all men. It teaches us to say "No" to ungodliness and worldly passions, and to live self-controlled, upright and godly lives in this present age (Titus 2:11-12; NIV).* So nobody is to blame when we make the wrong choices because God has given everyone a conscience to let them know right from wrong.

Because God has given all of us this moral compass we have a fair chance with the King even if we don't have a fair chance with the "system." The King's fair chance is more than the "system's" raw deal. When we are wronged, the King lifts us and makes the wrong become right. But some of us never learn that wrongdoing takes us down even when we have the best chance at making it—are the most likely to succeed. For this reason, many of my racial group are among the best talent, best sportspersons, best actresses, best entertainers, best scientists, and the best of everything. However, because we live a life of wrongdoing and getting one over on others, we take ourselves down so that those who otherwise would be among the best become the worst off. Doing right lifts us, but doing wrong takes us down.

Finally, I taught myself to obey Dr. Lightfoot's Recommended Six Lessons so I wouldn't suffer the consequences of the *Six Lessons Deficit.* Again, these lessons are:

- to close my mouth,
- to sit down and be still;
- to respect authority by being obedient/following instructions;
- to stand at/pay attention (keep my eyes on the teacher or task, later in life, paying attention helps you to keep your focus on your own business and not on other people to control, compare, or compete against them which will be trouble for you)

- to keep my hands and my mouth to myself, and
- to stay on task until I complete the job/task.

Big Mama would say all of this way, "Go sit down somewhere, close your mouth, pick up a book and read it, leave other folks alone and mind your own business." I made my life hard because I either wouldn't let my parents (grandparents) teach me or had no parents to teach me, but I was able to learn these Six Lessons because I was taught at school or at church when the church taught these lessons.

When I decided I needed to look at myself, unlearn wrong stuff, and work to change my bad-acting into acting right, I knew I had learned what my parents didn't teach me. So just because my parent did not teach doesn't mean I had no way of learning how to act because I still had my teachers at school and teachers at church. If I made excuses and took advantage of my teachers because I knew my parents were going to go against them even when I am wrong, I couldn't learn although my teachers were teaching me real good. I even know the State punishes the teachers when I fail to do my part; so I took advantage of this on this account but I was only hurting myself because my teacher already had her/his education and I had mine to get. Sadly, I oppressed myself but good news is whether our oppression was caused by someone else or by us, the King never fails and is always there to help us to change. He never leaves us but we leave Him!

When I started living for the King I learned to abide in Him through first inviting Him into my heart forever by praying, "Jesus, I invite You into my heart to dwell forever, to live in me and to shine through me, in Your name, Amen.

Whether you are or not thought to be a Roni, always remember, anyone can be a Roni, but you don't have to be one or act like one. Just know that Ronies make Ronies, and non-Ronies for the most part have nothing to do with the making, but benefit from the taking. We are our own worst enemy and must destroy our own internal evil of Roni-making by Roni-preachers, Roni-TV stars, and Roni-parents. Yet, even if we are ignorant, unlearned, unmotivated, trying to get one over, or poor, we don't deserve to be terrorized and murdered, we deserve to be loved and taught by instruction and example. Foremost, just because you started off as a Roni, doesn't mean you have to stay a Roni or a Roni-maker, because you have the power to choose to change your conduct and the King is right where you are to help you!

Before I go, let me give you the answer for all the problems we have with *us's* against *us's* and with them against *us's*. In a nutshell this book aims to get us to want to learn and grow by understanding what has happened to us to shake us from our roots of resilience, pride, and integrity. We've forgotten where we've come from, so we have no direction of where we should be going. We must understand that we are a people without a home, being sold into slavery by our own, being an outcast in America that pretends to accept us only that we can play sports, dance, make America laugh and sing for her when we are really targets of hatred and disparate treatment (known and unknown) that feeds into a self-fulfilling prophesy of the racial American stereotypes, loss of our racial identity, and our ways-of-life operating against us, which we have internalized and transmitted to each other causing us to forget whose we are, creating a preponderance of evidence that supports racial stereotypes of *us* among *us* and by *us* as a replacement of the former White slave master, both obvious and hidden in the collective consciences of HNIC's and White folks (and those who think they are White) that views the majority of us as all of us, resulting in all of us being treated as an overt threat to society and thereby controlled through Wrongful Collateral Damage and American Racist Terrorism.

This is the way it is going now, but we can change this if we'd go back to what we know works and that is living right! We were tricked by the Integration Disadvantage, and let white-folk teach us everything bad they know that they are now killing us for but we can take advantage of the Segregation Advantage and teach our people the truth because they are sitting up in our faces every Sunday. We are not any less than others and certainly are just as good as everyone else. Yet, we are worse off because of bad choices and we can change that, but we must first accept the truth about us in America: that we not equal. Big Mama taught me that we will always be considered niggers in America but must not ever forget because if we forget, white-folks will let us know that they think of us as less than. Therefore, we must do it three times better only to get less or the same. We will be the last hired and first fired, and if we go to the White-man's court we will not get fair or just treatment, but will be given cruel and unusual punishment, wrong punishment, and the maximum punishment for the same offenses committed by white-folks and white-want-to-be's." You must remember...

- ✓ You are not equal.
- ✓ You ain't got no rights.
- ✓ You will always be viewed as a nigger in America.
- ✓ You've got to be three times better to get less or the same, or better.
- ✓ Bad-acting black folks will make you believe the Six Rules in this book are wrong, but there is a zero tolerance for violators and if you break them, you will be made a slave without chains, locked up, or eliminated in America
- ✓ You are the last one hired and the first one fired.
- ✓ You will not be measured by the same yardstick as White-folks due to white privilege and racism.

178

✓ You will not likely get justice in the Whiteman's court, except by God's grace (BGG).
✓ The law was not initially made to help us but is more likely to work for us being under public scrutiny when we are in "the right."
✓ You will get the maximum penalty in the White-man's jail.
✓ You will receive cruel and unusual punishment and wrong punishment when you commit a crime.
✓ Your only hope out of poverty is getting a quality education, not a nothing degree; don't go the easy route— easy and quick don't last.
✓ Your only hope out of hell on earth and in eternity is a relationship with Jesus Christ.
✓ And, don't look for anybody because ain't nobody coming!
✓ But, if you are unable to do it or cannot do it yourself because you are permanently and totally disabled, we are supposed to help you and take care of you, so let us know and we will get you some help.

For these reasons, we need to do what's right because we need God on our side more than anything. The world hates us, but allows only a few of us excel to keep the rest of us in bondage and Roniland. We can break this if we make Roni skinny so Roni will not make it look like all of us are Ronies. I'm tired of getting blamed for what Roni does. I'm tired of White folks treating me like I'm a nigger and insulting, disrespecting, making us a scapegoat for American capitalism. There are many of us on welfare but there are plenty of white folk on welfare as well. I'm tired of White-folks insulting and killing us because Roni is so big and acts so bad, until they hate all of us. *But White-folks got Ronies too!* And as for the welfare system, it is to blame for teaching people to stay on it, when the system gives no incentive to get off and people don't have enough, the proper guidance, to use the system as a stepping-stone rather than a life-style. That's like blaming children for their parent's poor parenting. Let's stop low-rating the welfare recipients when the systems of capitalism, social welfare, and economics perpetuates the dependency and the culture of poverty associated with it. I went to school and followed all the rules and still was taken down by White-folks who saw me as an N-Word on a government job; so what does this say? We all wrongly suffer the wrongdoing of bad-actors who look like us and we suffer the wrongdoing of those who hate us.

Aren't you tired of this? Then let's turn this around by being the least at bad-acting, allowing our actions to shine over our appearance, and remove ourselves from Wrongful Collateral Damage and Racist Terrorism in America. We can do it, with God's help and He is right here to help us. He helps those who want to be helped. So come on, let's admit it, that we have rejected help and turned away from what we know is right.

Let's turn to the Help we have and pray, *"Father, God help me to want help and create in me a clean heart and renew the right spirit in me, so that I may know truth that will make me free. I need help to be what you made me to be--a good citizen who exemplifies the King--not who I learned to become and made myself to be--Roni! This I pray, in the name of Jesus Christ, our Lord, Amen!*

A turnaround is on the way for me! How about you? We can turn the tides against us in America if do it this way: understand how society view us in terms of racial prejudice, stop the fulfillment of racial stereotypes, change the worldview of ourselves, to receive treatment according to our acts not according to our appearance.

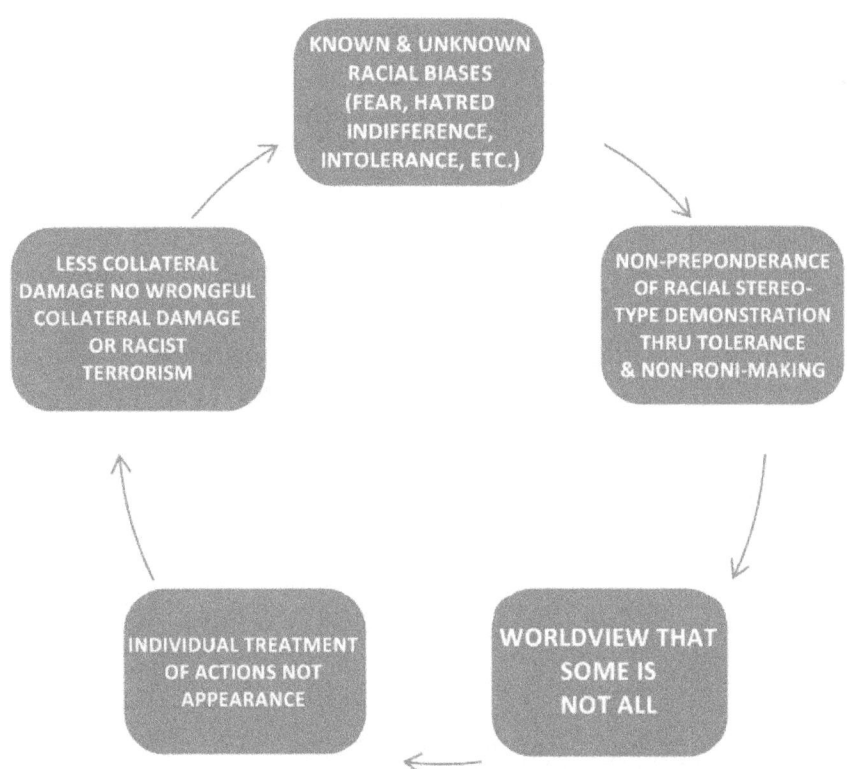

What happened to your elevator, Roni? *God gave it to ya, and you done gone and dropped it down low!* We know every tub has to sit on its own bottom and we've got to act right. Like I said, I was Roni, I love Roni, but I don't demonstrate Roni because God transformed with my best effort on His divine intervention.

If I can change anybody can. I was the best of bad-actors, specialized in bad-acting, and considered myself as the Queen of Low. I could get away with these things because like, Satan, I did it in secrecy. But, I don't live that way anymore. God helped me through friends and his power and not because of any good of my own. It was His grace that gave me the power to overcome. I just did the best I could which wasn't good enough, but God honored my best. I was down for many years, but I kept getting up. So, I know about the dual-reality of Roni-dom and the Kingdom, but I chose the Kingdom.[20] I know about Roni-mess and Roni-theology and how it deceives and shapes us into Roni for the benefit of bad-actors in charge. The way we carry-on in public is nothing but *embarrassing*. We don't have to live in Ronidumb but we just want to be dumb. We want to be slaves; we don't want freewill and are always looking for some dumb Roni-preacher to give us a word? For what? What's wrong with your bosom telephone? Can't you talk to God and know Him for yourself. All these Roni-preachers are doing is keeping us dumb for their own advantage because they know…

The dumber we come the softer we fall
and the more we can be controlled and used..

In falling soft we won't complain, we don't scream, and don't squirm even with a hirelings hands in our pants. Just dumb and want to be dumb? I don't understand. Even the so-called deacons are spineless and won't stand up to these wicked preachers saying, "Well he's the pastor," which is nothing more than saying, "He's the Master," because this system replaces slavery. These charlatans are doing nothing more than getting us ready for the jails and for hell and living low-down lives. Surely we're not learning anything from them; digesting hash and old trite church cliques and falling out and screaming over the same crap like, "Won't he do it," "He's good all the time," "I know he's alright!" This oppression is pitiful and has nothing to do what racism or 19th century slavery. We are doing this to ourselves. But we can wake-up and step-up to where life is good! We've had way more time to make it than the Hispanics, Asians, and Africans and it makes no sense for us to be where we are in America. We've got to step-up!

Knowledge really is power and when we know it, we can

---

[20] For the kingdom of God is not food and drink; but righteousness, and peace, and joy in the Holy Spirit (Romans 14:17; KJV).

change if we do not choose to ignore what we know. Thus, for Roni, knowledge is not enough because we must obey the learning that we know. And whenever we get ready to learn or when we have learning readiness, the teacher will show up and help us get the answer. It is then that we are empowered.

**Love God, Love ourselves, Do the work,
Do what's right to make black lives matter!**

Judge Lynn Toler, sums up the societal problem of Roni, on her July 6, 2015, Divorce Court filming, saying, "Let me tell You People something. Everybody has their limitations on how much disrespect they are going to take? Do you know about your issues? Do you know anything about the country that you live in? Do you know anything about what's happening today and about what Martin Luther King and my father and what all of those had to put up with in order to just keep us above ground? And you've got your limitations? My father had a degree, a doctorate in law and had to work in a linoleum factory just because he could not get a job in a law firm. He didn't have his limitations; he had his manhood; he had his obligations; he had what he needed to do; so he worked and he worked like a dog, put his daughters through school, because he was a man! What is the matter with you people? You can't just do whatever you want to; sleep with whomever you want to; have babies, praise Satan one day, go to church and think everything is going to be alright! You've got to make decisions; you've got to say, "I'm not allowed to do this; I'm not allowed to do that; I have to show self-respect; I've got to work; I'm not entitled to anything; I've got to work for everything. What are YOU PEOPLE doing? You've created a whole society of people who are absolutely incapable. No job skills, no ability, nothing to bring to the economy; you've got babies here and yonder; you've got no stability. What are we gonna do?"

CONCLUSION

Lastly, all lives matter, but since connotation is everything, people treat us according to how they see us whether what they see is true or false, right or wrong, good or bad. This applies to the treatment of black people as NWords in America which causes black people to be wrongly treated as if all black lives do not matter. However, I believe that black lives don't seem to matter in America firstly, because of racism and then secondly because of the misrepresentation of black people by NWords. There is a preponderance of visible evidence of bad-actors who look black, making all black people look like bad-actors or Nwords. Truth is that society has no place for people who do not love or respect themselves or others--NWords--other than jail and eradication. Thus, inherently black lives do matter but the target is on all Black people who are targeted as NWords. This target is laden with a mixed bag of rules, presenting unpredictable, favorable and unfavorable results. I experienced this on both sides, through racism and through "ronism" and it motivated me to write this book because collectively we must look at what we are doing to devalue our own lives and each other.

I've always been of the opinion that if you are not a part of the solution then you are a part of the problem. Therefore, I am becoming a part of the solution by making it clear that only until we demonstrate that we matter through the way we look collectively, only then will our lives matter collectively. We cannot merely say, "Black lives matter," but we must show it. No one is listening to what cannot be seen. I was so blinded by the connotation of "black misrepresented by bad-actors of similar physical characteristics" that my feelings about being black ranged from being shamed to being dissociated from my own racial identity for years until I went through a period of becoming one with myself as a person of color in a diverse world. I found that living among blacks with the high density of NWords was more taxing than living with racism. At least with racism there are laws to help to control violators. Whereas with Roni, your trauma is just left to internal and external emotional and economic suffering without recourse. This dual reality of racism and "ronism" forced me to come to terms with our "appearance of all effect," which I have resolved through writing this book.

I do not want to offend anyone, especially, my beloved people, but I had to say it. I had to bring the open-secret out of hiding. Matter of fact, we all know it, but no one wants to admit it. I understand saying it violates a custom, "Don't tell what goes on in this house," but this rule doesn't apply when abuse is present. So, I've said it, i.e., "We are the worst of the bad-actors, are doing it to ourselves, and need to step up." Therefore, I cannot keep this business in the house because to do so makes me privy to perpetuating self-abuse. Yes, we need to look better by acting better and we can with God's help." My passion and my calling is to reach those whom are thought of as less than, those who do not know who they are, those who have been given the wrong impression of who they are by those who teach them and provide role models for them, those who do not seem to matter, and those who are unrepresented in the minds of the masses--Roni. And I'll just keep running-on and telling the truth, 'cause that's the only way for us to be free. Let's face it, it's not slavery, it's not solely racism; it's primarily us that causes our lives not to matter! When we take our self-abuse out of the equation that goes against our value, then let's see what slavery and racism are doing? I'm not saying these factors have no negative effect on us, because they are real and they are cruel. But racism and slavery do not negatively affect our value. The negative effect on the value of our lives is associated with our actions demonstrated disproportionately in color, that outweighs the content of our character.

This book has been written to give our lives value by putting Roni-making on blast (to expose it/ to call someone/something out about something), in order to awaken my own people to God, because we are doing this to ourselves. We must stop looking at what "they" are doing and start looking at what "we" are doing to ourselves to make our lives not matter. We must show that our lives matter, not merely protest that they matter. Making our lives matter requires that we overcome the N-Word because we can't tell people to stop saying the N-Word or tell them to stop treating us like we are N-Words while they are still seeing the N-Word demonstrated by us. As harsh as it may sound, the state of affairs described herein are sadly true for many persons who face a double-dose of harsh perpetuation being "the system" and the "altered-self." May the exposure of "Roni-making by Ronies-In-Charge" cause this human-ill to decrease until it no longer exists. Of course, neither is the so-called educational nor the justice system trying to work itself out of a job; thus this leaves very few options for bad-actors to get real help. So, what do we do with Roni's terrorism on America? Hopefully, we will teach all people to respect others, themselves, and God by following the lessons in this book. Therefore this book is purposed give some real help to seekers of truth, to decrease the incidence of people being under educated and uneducated, to prevent people from falling into unjust legal systems, and to return the citizen to a God-fearing lifestyle. A God-fearing lifestyle is the only quality that will make Black lives matter.

Finally, this is my prayer for you and me:

Father, God, Jehovah I pray:

May we invite Jesus Christ into our hearts to dwell forever,

May those in law enforcement, government, television, and community leadership be guided by the Holy Spirit to show the love, wisdom and knowledge of God; we need truth in the inward soul,

May we always be little in our own eyes to always recognize our need for God,

May the blessing of God be upon us,

May His peace be with us,

May His presence enlighten our hearts and walk,

Both now and forever more, in the name of Jesus Christ, the King, I pray with thanksgiving,
Amen.
Lovingly,
Dr. Jan

Truth is: I Don't Like You Either
Maybe some people don't like you
'cause of the color of your skin,
The quality of your character any barrier can transcend,
Don't think that it's just a matter of group preference,
I've got news for you,
You see, I don't like you either 'cause you don't love yourself.

You say you know who you are, but you have no identity,
Fighting with strangers over and over again,
bad-actors on the TV,
Tearing up your neighborhood;
taking jobs from your own selves,

There are Other Black Sons to Save

Your actions speak louder than your words;
so if you matter, stop raising hell.

To know yourself is to love yourself but others pull your strings,
You say I'm my own person,
but you don't know what that means,
You think it's you, who controls your acts?
I've got news for you,
I know you don't know who you are
when you don't control what you do.

You won't go to school,
You won't follow rules,
You act just like a fool,
What's the matter with you?
You don't respect the rights of others,
Don't regard brothers as brothers,
You don't live in this world alone,
I'm tired of being disturbed by you in my home.

I don't like you either,
But I still LOVE you,
No! I don't like you either,
But I still LOVE you,
I don't like you either,
Cause you don't love yourself.
PS: And your life won't even matter,
Until you matter to yourself!
                    J Lightfoot

Bye for Now! This is my last ditch effort to save Ronies from Ronies; I'm going atop this crawfish bowl, go with the goers and let Roni be damned if this is what Roni chooses to do. I've done all I can do and I'll leave the results to God, but at least I've tried. Always remember, we are valuable, we deserve to be loved, respected, and taught, but we must also be teachable. I have tried to teach us what we've forgotten, so that we may return to a place of resilience and respectability. We are "a freed people with an incarcerated mind," but need not be. We do not have to buy into the church's indoctrination of no standards through the cheapening of God's grace; we don't have to buy into our so-called leaders indoctrination of making excuses and blaming others, and we need not buy into government's indoctrination of protection and freedom. Our only freedom is in Christ. When we relearn and obey the truth we have learned we will turn away from Roni-making and Roni-acting that leads us to self-destruction, then we can receive God's protection because when we love God we are in the world but not of it because we dwell in Him (Psalms 91). Remember............

> *Righteousness exalts a nation, but sin is a disgrace even to the best of any people (even us). The King's favor is toward a servant who acts wisely, but his anger is toward him who acts shamefully—us.* (Proverbs 14: 34 & 35: NASB & Author Paraphrase).

I followed this path and it worked for me and if I did it anybody can; 'cause I way behind the starting line before my race ever got started, but I did what Big Mama said, "Do what's right and listen to God and He will bless you!" So Godspeed with this because I see great potential in us!

**Lastly, Black lives will matter when
God matters to Black Lives!**

Definitions

Ability to Move Around: Power of the feet to relocate an individual from a bad place to a good place through independence rather than dependence.

African-American-Misnomer: The wrong name ascribed to Black Americans, that is also an oxymoron (or impossible and false reality) given to and accepted by Americans with African Roots/Americans of Negroid Blood; this wrong name creates a displaced identity crisis of not being connected to any group, purpose, or land; also it creates a disadvantage solely for the benefit of the larger society and the elite.

American Racist Terrorism: Ideologies and practices in America that seek to justify and carry out inciting fear within and performing violence against a particular racial group--Blacks. In America these ideas of White Supremacy permeate the collective conscience and are tolerated as norms of American society.

Appearance of All Effect: Such a high demonstration of certain characteristics and attributes observed in a group, giving the appearance that all persons of that group are of the same characteristics and attributes. The all effect is never true because one deviation defies it; yet it is treated as a generalized truth.

Black-on-Black Ignorance: The dual practice of those who know failing to teach and those who do not know inability to teach. Both cause us to transmit ignorance and give faulty knowledge to ourselves, i.e., know but will not and don't know and cannot.

Black-White American Divide: The war in America between black people and white supremacists ideology resulting in the dispensing of terror upon Black people by white supremacists (whites, policeman, bullies, vigilantes, bigots, haters, racists) and the return of terror upon white supremacists by Blacks, with both side having been put in terror of each other among and by each other.

"C" Word Discrediting Game: To call someone "crazy" in order to make them a character flaw and to discredit what they know, say, have accomplished, or to make their good of no effect so that they are silenced and/or unseen. This is related to the invalid societal stigma upon mental-illness making mental illness the most disrespected of all conditions although this condition is neither a choice nor self-inflicted.

Certain People: A code word and alternate name for the N-Word and Roni, which is not a look, but an *act*. It refers to any race, creed, or kind or people who have no love and/or respect for themselves and others, undergirded by a "don't-give-a-care attitude. This code word presents a more politically correct expression of an offensive expression, as does the expression, Roni.

Collateral Damage: The unintentional killing, injuring, and terrorizing of people through action designed for an intended target whereas the unintended target is hurt due to targeting a few and getting some.

Collective Conscience or Collective Conscious: What the populace believes in awareness and unawareness cooperatively, together, or as a whole.

College Bound Launch: The option of using public, private, and higher education to move yourself into success by you first taking responsibility to be your first teacher who accepts all other teachers who will teach you and by using available tools, books, and teachers to help yourself to become successful because the educational system is failing to educate.

Cooling Board Lynch: The option of allowing public, private, and higher education to move you into poverty, crime, and failure by your refusal use educational tools and true teachers to help you to teach yourself.

Covert or Triple Threat: An unobservable quality whereby the individual or group that does right by themselves, others, and God is empowered to be adept in all areas of life whereby one is untouchable, protected, or able to be defended against American racism, abuse, and hatred.

Crude Talk/Teaching/Therapy: The use of profane language, subtle threats of rejection, insults against one's core values, along with projecting a "go to hell/nonchalant" attitude to the recipient of the talk/teaching/therapy in order to speak the language the person understands and meet them where they are and lift them to where they belong.

Equalization Plan: God's plan for the individual to rise above what he or she is in through individual action rather than group appearance/performance; so that the individual who lives Godly gains favor with God and man that allows him/her to have success regardless of his/her challenges or the political climate because God's equality beats man's inequality.

Exclusive Black Production: The lone acts that Black America does against each other to keep its own group down, poor, and oppressed that has nothing to do with White America.

Exterminate Without Discrimination: The Order of the Day in America to Kill All Black People (more accurately named American Citizens of Negroid Blood, Persons of Negroid Blood, People/Americans of African descent, wrongly named African Americans) and to Kill All Black People by making no distinction in favor of or against, a Black person based on the Appearance (color) of all of the group, class, or kind to which a Black person belongs, versus making a distinction on individual merit and this order produces the killing of and ill treatment of all Black persons.

Failed Relocation Solution: The attempt of an irresponsible person move to another location to solve a problem without having the necessary living arrangements (a job, a home, or a car) but the move fails because the person is taking the problem with them—their head.

Freedom from Roni: Knowledge that brings emotional and financial independence thereby giving US the power to move away from and discard persons, places, and things that make us unhappy.

Good Etiquette: Correct ways of life that have been proven by being passed down through generations which have general agreement as to the most peaceful and cordial ways to live with most people cross-culturally. God's Word: Bible truth that God has said and inspired.

GYOSY (Geeosy): A neologism for *Get Yo Own Stuff Yourself* from someone who is saying, "I am not willing to and not going to give you my stuff; so *Gyosy*...and this meaning getting it the right way. GYOSYN (Get Yo Own Stuff Yourself N......) may be necessary for certain people to hear before they get it that you are not giving them your money.

Injustice Avoidance: To abide by the law and consequently avoid the injustice of the law.

Integration Deception: The gray or the loss of Black family values, work ethics, and God-fearing practices through the mixing of Blacks and Whites in integration that resulted the lies that all people are equal, which we are not; that all people have rights, which we do not have; and that truth changes with the situation, which it does not. Thus, integration has served as our worst social and spiritual enemy.

I.D. or Integration Disadvantage: The forgetting of *Five Truths of existence for Americans of African Descent* to a disadvantage, which are, that: (1) We are not equal and must live with a unequal-double standard; (2) We will be the last hired and first fired; (3) We have to be 3-4 times better to achieve the same or less; (4). We must do the right thing and God will be on our side; (5) When we do wrong we will get the max penalty in the court and our parents are not going to pay any money to get you off or out because when crime is the choice you make then time is the price you pay. We lost our way through integration.

Learning Readiness: When an individual makes the choice to learn or to be taught by unlearning what they think they know and relearning what they need to know causing a teacher to show up in body and/or in spirit because, "When the student gets ready to learn, the Teacher will show up!"

Looking Good-Acting Bad Disparity: Inconsistency between the way one looks and behaves because of a focus on rich-looking clothing and an ignoring of poor conduct.

Lopsided Appearance of All Deception: Blindness that is caused by a high demonstration of certain characteristics and attributes observed in a group, giving the appearance that all persons of that group are of the same characteristics and attributes. This leads to racial and other types of profiling—targeting people according to a racial stereotype.

Mixed Bag of Rules: The reality that for the same right action Blacks are treated negatively or condemned from that of whites who are commended for the same right action. This also applies to the same wrong action wherein Whites are rewarded and Blacks are punished. This also explains white privilege.

Mutual Intervening Fear: A real fear that exists in a member of the minority race group associated with the unfair treatment of the minority racial group member that all persons of that group are subject to suffer whether blameworthy or not together with a real fear existing in White policemen causing a mutual fear reaction of primarily non-verbal provocation that results in wrongful collateral damage against that member of the minority racial group, i.e., the clash of fear between Black people and White police that places Black people in harm of deadly force from White policemen.

My own business: To attend to one's own needs, problems, success, and responsibilities, not looking to, at, and around others competing, comparing, becoming discouraged, but continuing little by little until little becomes much because little becomes much in the King's hand.

N-Word: Nigger (A person of any race, creed, or kind who does not respect or love themselves, others, authority figures, or God).

Nonverbal-Provocation: The lack of verbal language and the occurrence of nonverbal communication in gestures, bodily movements, facial expressions, breathing patterns, or any visible reaction interpreted in varying degrees of violence in accordance with one's own biases that provoke a hostile reaction.

Order of the Day: Manifestation of a collective desire or the reality of a collective desire underlying a collective mindset in America which directs society to take a certain action--this refers to the present-day societal approval of killing all Black people without discrimination or without distinguishing the good from the bad.

Overt Threat: An observable quality whereby the individual or group that does not do right by themselves, others, and God is powerless in being adept in all areas of life whereby one is touchable, unprotected, or unable to be defended against American racism, abuse, and hatred.

Paid Verbiage: When you are not free to say what is true or what you would like to say because your audience has control over your pocket and will hold back your money if and when you displease them; you are paid to talk, but you must say what your audience wants you to say.

Pantywaist: A man who is weak, irresponsible, unmanly, and pathetic.

Right-Way vs. the White-Way: The two options for our actions with the Right-Way being to do what is right on your own with dignity, versus the White-Way being to do it by force with disgrace.

Roni: Pet name, lovingly substituted for the N-Word and the prototype of "a sinner" and a euphemism--an indirect, or mild expression presented as a replacement for the N-Word in consideration of the harshness and offensiveness of this word, fondly coined by the author and referred to as a "nickname" to soften the blow of the N-Word in order to offer a lesson in overcoming the N-Word, and to express my love for Roni.

Roni-dom: An author invented word expressing a literal and figurative reality only in the earth realm that destroys a *life* that gives joy and peace, destroys *hope* that gives determination, and destroys *truth* that gives protection and freedom.

Roni-Ignorance: A thinking pattern which makes the choice to ignore what is known to be true and right in favor of following one's own way that is false and wrong together with the refusal to own the choice or take responsibility for the choice, thus placing oneself in the position of never learning from wrong choices which results in making oneself a threat to and a burden upon society.

Roni-Breaking: The practice of benefitting in a malevolent way from the disadvantages of people who have been conditioned into satisfying racial stereotypes or malevolent prejudice and mistreatment against a member of a racial group according to racial stereotypes for which the targeted individual has not demonstrated.

Roni-Making: The practice of conditioning people to satisfy negative racial stereotypes, helplessness, purposeful suffering, false hope, and victimization.

Segregation Advantage: The missed opportunity by Black leaders to raise Biblical awareness in a holistic way--body, mind, and spirit—that results in a false belief system that lacks demonstration of a positive impact upon the lives of their listeners—Ex: Missing in Action Belief System.

Self-Education or Teaching: A necessary ingredient for receiving an education in today's world is not to look to anyone or any system to teach you and to rely on yourself to teach yourself through reading and to receive competent teaching where it can scarcely be found knowing that you have an Internal Teacher who knows all, sees all, and teaches all.

Self-Inflicted Zeroed-out Effect: An unconscious belief in the individual and collective conscience of a person and people that binds them to behavior that demonstrate the lack of love for themselves, others, and a higher power. Unconscious and conscious belief that I/we am/are nothing to ourselves.

Self-Perpetuated-Culture of Ignorance, Bad-acting, and Poverty: Self-Perpetuated Culture of Ignorance, Bad-acting, and Poverty: What happens within a group by the group and against itself to bring itself down through learned, shared, and transmitted self-defeating beliefs that translates into within group behavior based on these beliefs resulting in stereotypical behavior that threatens the larger society and the group themselves.

Six Lessons Deficit: Our Failure to teach and learn to: (1) close your mouth, (2) sit down quietly, (3) follow instructions, (4) stand at/pay attention (keep eyes on task/teacher), (5) keep your hands and mouth to myself and (6) complete the task/job, and this deficit amounts to a general disrespect for authority causing us to suffer mistreatment, abuse, racism and brutality.

Stir and Study: To perform the gifts and talents that we inherently possess (stir), but to also develop and maximize these gifts and talents through formal and academic study areas related to them (study).

Subculture: Ways of life and the artifacts identified in groups as indigenous behavior within and aspects of that particular group that goes against or threatens the larger society.

System-Perpetuated-Culture of Ignorance, Bad-Acting, and Poverty: What happens outside of a group to bring it down with use of the group itself to camouflage racism (Roni-making) that the larger group uses to oppress the minority group. This is what thought-to-be respected social systems (educational, religious, governmental) do so, to predict polices and decisions that condition and keep a certain racial group at a financial, social, moral and educational disadvantage in a way that goes against and threatens the larger society and the oppressed racial group.

Target or Identification Blindness: The inability to discern a difference between a citizen and a criminal of the Black race due to racial prejudice against the color of one's skin rather than an evaluation of the demonstration of his/her character due to the unconscious and conscious belief that, "Everything black is a Nigger," causing Black people to be treated (by society in general and by persons in authority) as if all Black people are criminals to include Black people who are law-abiding citizens, subjecting all Black people to societal ill treatment and the endangerment of Wrongful Collateral Damage by authority figures with badges and guns, bigots, racists, and haters.

Terminal Degree: A degree which provides a conferee with qualifications to meet the standards of job demand in that field of study. For example, the terminal degree in Psychology and Sociology is a PhD, RN a Bachelor's degree, Social Work a Master of Social Work, Teaching a Bachelor's Degree with a Teaching Certification; Accountant a MBA. You should know what the educational needs are to meet the needs of the job market's demand and supply, which without you can very well earn a degree that will NOT land you a good job but cause you to yet owe excessive student loans for that you cannot afford to repay.

The 80-90 Theory: The existence wherein the largest numbers of a racial group (up to 80%) are people who neither love or respect themselves or others and this largest percentage is also comprised of an even larger percentage (up to 90%) of the same type of persons who attend church and are religious, but are not Christ-followers. This subjects Black American citizens to a double fight internally (the subculture—Ronies) and externally (the larger culture—Racism).

The Gray: A existence whereby in unawareness an individual and/or group is oppressed by what they believe is liberating them creating a mindset whereby the individual or group submits to predictions and policies that eliminate their opportunity for equal access to opportunity.

The Key: Righteousness or (a right relationship with God through accepting and following Jesus Christ) is the one thing that will open the door to beating the odds against any foe, individual, and or system.

The King: Jesus Christ who is our Internal Teacher and our door to oneness with God.

The Kingdom: A literal and figurative reality in earth and eternity which gives us Life, Hope, and Truth. Life gives us peace and joy, Hope gives us determination, and Truth gives is protection and freedom.

The Light: The ability of all persons to overcome darkness through obeying God by following the example of Jesus Christ that brings truth, love, and light.

The Lopsided Effect: Disproportionate numbers of bad acting within-group that feeds into an appearance of all in bigoted and ethnocentric individuals causing the entire group to look the same. For example, when 80 - 90% of within-group behavior results in an appearance of all of that group.

The N-Word: Euphemism for the word, 'Nigger," which has dual meaning as it relates to the object (an appearance) and to a behavior (an action) with both positive and negative connotations among Americans of African Descent with African Roots and other racial groups. Positively it refers to an object or to an admired person and is fondly referred to; also referred to as Nigga. It refers to anyone who demonstrates a lack of respect for oneself, others, or God, meaning it is not racially based but focuses on behavior. In Society it is a wrong and negative construct of Black people based on appearance or skin color and represents the entire group of Americans of African Roots regardless of a demonstration of identifying behavior (ex: Everything Black is a nigger). The negative and positive use varies from person to person and has inconsistent use/meaning (example, "You're a cold nigger," is a compliment among AAD's whereas, "You're a low nigger," is an insult).

Trump Terror: Extreme fear, horror with trembling, alarm and panic in a traumatizing way within American collective conscience, caused by Donald Trump's display of disrespect, lack of empathy and understanding, and poor boundaries, presenting him as a bad-actor and a terror--one who causes terror, trouble, fighting, social unrest, hatred and disrespect for God, others, and himself. Moreover, although denied/ignored, this ever-present and overweening phenomenon is the elephant in the room.

Unbrainwash: The need for relearning by certain persons who have been falsely indoctrinated to become "other directed" in their focus regarding their own lives allowing them to have feelings of entitlement, feelings of helplessness, feelings of blaming, and feelings of ingratitude, to render them irresponsible, unresponsive, and abusive to themselves and others.

White Privilege: A favoritism or advantage that fortifies whites and white-skinned people against rightful scrutiny, racism, discrimination, prejudices, unfairness, as well as, giving them protection from legal accountability for wrongdoing and this privilege that is not experienced by non-whites under the same legal, social, political, and economic conditions. Prime example: Donald Trump winning the 2016 US Presidential Election and Bill Cosby being taken to zero.

White Supremacy (from dictionary.com): The belief, theory or doctrine that white people are inherently superior to people from other racial groups, especially black people, and are therefore rightfully the dominant group in any society who should dominate society.

World of True Knowledge and Excellence: A quality and requirement of the larger social order nullified by the present false knowledge taught in the educational system not made available to students who fail to take responsibility for gaining a quality education for themselves.

Wrongful-Collateral-Damage: The wrongful and intentional killing, injuring, and terrorizing of people through action by and through the so-called justice system and members of society in the course of maintaining law and order due to targeting the whole and getting some.

Poetic Insights

Everything Black Ain't a Nigger!

I went to a Chick-fil-A,
So-called Christians so they say,
Could a been shot by a bully cop,
Who went into a color-blind rage,
He yelled, "You don't look disabled,
Ain't nothing wrong with you,
I'm tired of you people parking here;
This is my job to do,"
I cried, "Sir this is my placard,
You're welcome to check my license plate,"
But he'd already decided to treat me like a nigger,
So he wouldn't hear what I had to say,
So, I'm singing to Chick-fil-a,
Calling yourselves Christians by the way,
Smiling so sweet; but no help at all,
Talking Jesus, but not walking his way,
You need to know...

    Everything black ain't a nigger,
    Everything black ain't a threat,
    Everything black ain't a nigger,
    So don't put a target on my back.

    Some of US may be bad actors,
    Every group has their own share,
    But just because we are the same color,
    Don't put US all in the same class.

Everything black ain't a nigger,
Everything black ain't a threat,
Everything black ain't a nigger,
So don't put a target on my back.

We may look lopsided,
With bad-actors being the most,
But don't put us all together,
Separate the sheep from the goats!

Everything black ain't a nigger,
Everything black ain't a threat,
Everything black ain't a nigger,
So don't put a target on my back.

A bird is black... (you ain't trying to kill that)
A horse is black... (you ain't trying to kill that)
A bear is black... (you ain't trying to kill that)
A dog is black... (you ain't trying to kill that).

Ludicrous to say, "You're doing your job,"
When you are terrorizing and killing us,
Getting away with it like with Freddie Gray,
While we're making y'all rich buying chicken every day,
Killing niggers making y'all rich every day,
Buying cheap clothes and chicken from CFA,
Don't get it twisted; that Black means nigger,
All of us don't dance in the streets and jigger,
We learned good manners and how to work,
All of us are not trying to get over and shirk...
I own my stuff and can move around,
Not looking for nothing free; I cover my ground,
Wasn't trying to park in the space for free,
If I was a white lady, you wouldn't have bothered me,

 You need to know...
Everything black ain't a nigger,
Everything black ain't a threat,
Everything black ain't a nigger,
So don't put a target on my back,
So don't put a target on my back,
So don't put a target on my back.

Conscience: Get You Some Act Right!

Get you some act right, to make it in this world,
Get you some do right, no excuses boys and girls,
You might not have a teacher,
To look at with your eyes,
But you have a teacher,
Who lives down inside.

Get you some act right, to keep the white man off your back,
Get you some do right, to keep Satan off your track,
You might not have a teacher,
To look at with your eyes,
But you have a teacher,
Who lives down inside.

Listen to the voice,
And make the right choice,
You've got an elevator,
Let the Lord take you up,
You might not, have a teacher,
To look at with your eyes,
But you have a teacher,
Who lives down inside!

Get you some act right, to make it in this world,
Get you some do right, no excuses boys and girls,
You might not have a teacher,
To look at with your eyes,
But you have a teacher,
Who lives down inside.

Act right, do right, dress right, speak right,
Act right, do right, dress right, speak right!
Reach for it,
Reach for it,
Reach for it,
Reach for it,
You might not have a teacher,
To look at with your eyes,
But you have a teacher,
Who lives down inside,
Reach for it,
Reach for it,
Reach for it,
Reach for it.

Even if your mother and father forsake you,
Then the Lord will take you up (repeat).
If my mother and father forsake me, then the Lord will take me
up!
Act right, do right, dress right, speak right!
Reach for it!

Everybody Must Respect Authority

Everybody's got to learn, to respect authority,
If you won't hear Mama & Daddy, you're gonna hear somebody,
Society can't let people, do whatever they want to do,
Everybody must respect the power, so things can go smooth,
It's all about social control, so everybody won't suffer for a few,
People who have no respect, must be silenced and incarcerated,
This is the only way, for a thriving world, to be elevated,
When it comes to authority, we have no vote or opinion,
Know when to close your mouth, and when to speak; the law still
has dominion,
Don't try to run things, when you ain't in charge there,
And know when to go sit down somewhere!

Are you too stupid to understand, ain't nobody playing with you?
Society won't sacrifice the whole for a few,
They'll lose a few bad cops and vigilantes, to hold you at bay,
But nobody cares about what you have to say,
Living in terror that any day, you might be coming our way,
So we just turn our heads declaring OMG!
But we're glad, somebody is keeping you away,
If your life really matters, you've got to show some sign,
Stop acting a fool, in the streets, making trouble, showing your
behinds.

They are killing you, to hold you at bay, because you have no
respect,
Killing and looting in the streets, is doing nothing but making
things worse,
Hysteria on the TV about the police killing blacks, is only a ploy
to pacify the situation,
Ain't nobody really paying you no mind, because violence
against you is necessary, to save the nation,

You can't make folks believe your life matters, while showing them your behind,

Keep your business out of the street, go to court, talk is cheap,

You need to show some sign,

You never learned to respect authority, at all,

First and foremost because, you never learned to close your big mouth,

Two wrongs don't make it right, but you ain't in charge,

Learn protocol and cut it out!

And stop going to jail, complaining about being done wrong,

When you have no business, going there at all,

Tax payers ain't paying for your comfort,

Cause you don't have enough sense to leave people and their stuff alone,

You have a second chance to be taught at school,

Even if your parents didn't teach you at home,

Secondly, you never learned to go sit down, keep still, and pay attention,

So you don't even know what's going on, even when it's mentioned,

Thirdly, your brain follows your eyes; so you need to pay attention to your own affairs,

Keeping your eyes on your own paper, and your mouth on your own plate,

Is the first order of business, where you need to concentrate,

Now the only remedy for the resolute disrespect of authority, is a bullet to the head,

But they don't have to do that, all they've got to do is to let you shoot yourself in the foot, then leave you for dead,

So, don't just say, "Black lives matter," when you refuse to show it,

You need to act like you matter, if you want the world to know it,

Your action speaks louder, than your words,

We cannot see what cannot be heard!

Action speaks louder than words,
Get you some act right, if you want to be heard,
If your life matters, you need to show some sign,
Get out of the streets, showing your behind,
Go to court, where you can have a voice,
Stop the violence, and make the right choice,
Since action speaks, louder than words,
We cannot see, what cannot be heard,
Don't just say, "Black lives matter," when you refuse to show it,
You need to act like you matter, if you want the world to know it,
Action speaks louder than words,
We cannot see what cannot be heard!

I Won't Give Up On Man

I won't give up on man,
I'm not satisfied where we stand,
We've got to stop getting over and start to love again,
I won't give up on man.

Love lift us up where we belong,
Where the eagles fly on a mountain high,
We've got to stop getting over and start to love again,
I won't give up on man.

No man is an island,
No man stands alone,
Each man's joy is joy to me,
Each man's grief is my own,
We've got to stop getting over and start to love again,
I won't give up on man.
My country 'tis of thee,

Sweet land of liberty,
Of thee I sing,
Land where my father's died,
Land of the pilgrim's pride,
From every mountain side, let freedom ring.

We must shout it from the mountaintop,
To let the world know,
We've got to stop getting over and start to love again,
I won't give up on man.

I won't give up on man,
I'm not satisfied where we stand,
We've got to stop getting over and start to love again,
I won't give up on man.

Wolves In Sheep's Clothes

I heard the story of Jesus; it sounded so good to me,
I heard the story of Jesus; I believe he can set me free,
But I fear I could not stand, the deeds of a wicked preacher man,
That would bind my soul to the fires of eternal hell.

I know the Lord saved me; but I need a new church home,
I've grown beyond where I am; it's time to find a new home,
But I fear I could not stand, the deeds of a wicked preacher man,
That would bind my soul to the fires of eternal hell.

It's hard to be a seeker, when you don't know what to do,
It's hard to be a seeker, when you don't know what is true,
When you are looking for the Lord, knowing his voice is so hard,
Wolves in Sheep clothes, God don't like it!

Priest and preachers you ought to be ashamed,
For playing that awful money game,
Making the church a free-for-all, barely working at all,
You've made the church a despicable thing,
Because it's just a money game,
Wolves in Sheep clothes, God don't like it!

It's hard to be a seeker,
When preachers don't practice what they preach,
It's hard to be a seeker,
When priest don't perform what they teach,
You've got to answer for your sin; Jesus is coming back again,
Wolves in Sheep clothes, God don't like it!

Priests and preachers fleece the flock,
Men of God there ain't a lot,
Priest and preacher fleece the flock,
Men of God there ain't a lot,
They nothing but wolves in sheep's clothes,
And God don't like it,
Wolves in sheep's clothes.

On The Church

Fact is, I dislike the church but I love God,
Cause it's all we've got though it sucks,
The same I say of family, husbands, and America,
Cause the best we got ain't enough,
Our faulty systems make me sick,
Cause the ego leads over true spirit,
Conscience is put on the back burner,
While we ignore stuff and sear it,

So I'll keep raining on everyone's party,
Saying stuff nobody wants to hear in their ears,
Because just because we're right for what we're thinking,
Don't mean what we're looking at is what it says it is!
Church hurt, is the worse hurt,
I ain't going to church, to get hurt no more,
Church hurt, is the worse hurt,
I'll meet Jesus, on the other shore!

Decoy (written by the Author's son)

I'm a decoy for the popo, Mama, 'cause of the color of my skin.

I'm a decoy for the popo, Mama, I'm a nigger and I just can't win,

Mama, you said, "Son, get your sticker so you won't get pulled on the side of the road!"

Mama, it don't matter if my sticker is good or bad, I'm still carrying a heavy load.

My skin is a decoy for the popo and enticement that I just can't hide,

Being a Black man in America is nothing but a thorn in my side.

"Oh son, it makes me ever so sad to know that you feel this way,

I told your Daddy we shouldn't bring kids into this dreadful world of war and hate.

Son, I'm sorry for bringing you into a world where your starting line is behind the rest.

Mama loves you and wants you to know, you are just as good as the best of the best.

If I could've made the choice I would've made sure that you were a little girl,

'Cause I know how hard it is for a Black man to make it in this cruel world."

Racial profiling, busted for styling, makes my body a freaking trap,

Last hired, first fired, wrong color to be good at what I do,

I'm sick and tired of this crap.

Whether I'm intelligent or dumb,

I'm a know-it-all nigger or an Uncle Tom!

Can't get a break no matter what I do, caught in a double bind,

Doesn't matter if I work or go to school; it's enough to make me lose my mind!

I'll always be a nigger no matter how high I climb, and I'd better never forget that fact,

'Cause as soon as I think I've arrived, the White man will say nigger step back!

White is still right and Black git out of sight is still the way it goes,

White is supreme and Black is demeaned is the road the social order shows.

Mama, you went to college, graduated cum laude, only for the system to take you down.

How can I sing God bless America after America turned yo smile into a frown?

And worst of all is knowing wherever I go I'm a target because of my outer shell.

Being a Black man in America ain't nothing but a doggone living hell.

Dr. King did many good things to bring all men justice and liberty,

Still the Black male suffers racial hatred in America to a great degree.

There's nothing worse than living in fear of knowing anytime I'll be discriminated against without grounds,

While everybody just goes on doing business as usual as the system takes my butt down.

Trapped in a covering of indelible skin that leads to me into danger,

And everybody wants to know why's a nigga so filled with apathy and anger?

If I could'a chose who I would've been, I would'na made my body a freaking trap,

That lures trouble right to my front door and gives me a whole bunch of crap!

"Oh Son . . . boo . . . hoo . . . Don't feel like you're a decoy!

Lord, please have mercy. Don't let America destroy my baby boy! Waa waa!"

I'm a decoy for the popo, Mama, 'cause of the color of my skin.

I'm a decoy for the popo, Mama, I'm a nigger and a just can't win.

Paree' Christophe

How Does It Feel When Disrespect Meets With Disrespect?

How does it feel to have a job you can't quit?
When you've got to get up when you don't want to?
And put your walk with your talk?
I know what that's like and I'd rather be rid of it,
'Cause a 50-50 split is not a win; it's a divided house,
Which against itself cannot stand; no surprise to me,
That what kills Pharaoh's army, saves Abraham's seed,
I'm glad I know Whom to reverence--God alone!
This world is not my hope and certainly not my home,
And that anyone can be one who neither loves or respects,
But yet, ...I live under the shadow of the Almighty,

Untouched by those who live with this utter regret,
Where talk is cheap but working it is another story,
I'll keep watching y'all fight about only God knows what?
As I go on joyfully sheltered and growing from glory to glory.

God is Greater Than Trump

I'm not afraid; I trust in the Lord,
I will not fear; I trust in His Word,
The angel of the Lord, encamps around me,
To protect me and keep me from all harm,
Though I walk through the valley of the shadow of death,
I will not fear any evil,
I trust in His Word.
If God be for us, who can be against us?
Sopranos: Fear no evil;
Altos: God's not given us the spirit of fear,
Tenors: God is greater than Trump...........

Epilogue

I've got helping in me, and that's OK,
But I've overstepped what are proper bounds,
Allowing my helpfulness to try to help bad actors,
Costing me more than it cost them cause they wanted a free ride,
I was so much into fixing my own hurt through everyone else,
Until I didn't realize that I was really trying to fix me,
Problem is you can't anybody who doesn't want to be helped,
So in desperation I tried to undo being rejected by my own flesh,
Rather than accepting what lies in my flesh—contradiction,
That cannot be fixed in this body, only in my resurrected body,
Because it was my own mother, who made me zero to myself,
So I tried playing savior, when there is only One—Jesus Christ!
And the only place for me on this side of life is in His grace,
I've had to look at "Why" and "How" I do what I do?
Am I helping someone for themselves or more for me?

When helping them for me,
I'm trying to help void of God's grace,
Because in my troubles I didn't see Him or His grace,
So after seeing His grace, when helping them for themselves,
I'm walking beside them in His grace,
Because I have become a partaker of grace,
I now understand what the Bible means when it says,
*"I tell you that to everyone who has, more will be given, but as
for the one who has nothing, even what he has will be taken away*
(Luke 19:26; NIV)," God gives us the grace to sink or swim,
Thus, I need not feel guilty or repentant or feel unworthy,
That I have received His grace where I am weak and empty,
Because all of us have a place of strength in His cross,

217

He gives grace to the weak and in our weakness,
His strength is made perfect, as I lived and learned for me,
I've done wrong by trying to be in control of my salvation,
My purpose, my destiny, God's business,
and the same for others,
But now I have learned to walk in the strength of Jesus,
Comfortable in my rejecting-of-me flesh that renders me zero,
So, I now release my burden of Roni to God!
Amen

I know we are living in a terrorizing time, but take heart because God has not left us. He is even married to the backslider. However, we need not continue to open ourselves up for trouble but receive the protection of the Almighty through submission to the will of God shown through living right in God's strength because righteous will lift us but our unrighteousness is bringing us down.

WORKS CITED

A Conversation With My Friend (Darryl Staggers); (March 7, 2015 via telcon).

A Freed People With An Incarcerated Mind, Sermon Topic, By Rev. Jerome Stinson @ Cornerstone Community of Faith Church, November 20, 2016; Dr. B. Wesley Austin, Jr., Pastor; Houston, TX.

Black Lives Matter Website: (n.d.). Retrieved September 3, 2016, from http://blacklivesmatter.com/ BlackLivesMatter is an online forum intended to build connections between Black people and our allies to fight anti-Black racism, to spark dialogue among Black people, and to facilitate the types of connections necessary to encourage social action and engagement.

CBS News. Baltimore mom: "I just lost it" seeing son at riots with rock in hand. (2015, April 29). Retrieved September 11, 2016, from http://www.cbsnews.com/news/baltimore-mom-toya-graham-on-smacking-son-at-riots-freddie-gray/

Collateral Damage Defined; Scribendi Editor Comments, March 2015.

Hersholt, J. (n.d.). THE EMPEROR'S NEW CLOTHES. Retrieved July 22, 2016, from http://andersen.sdu.dk/vaerk/hersholt/TheEmperorsNewClothes_e.html

Juzwiak, R., and Chan, A. (2014, December 08). Unarmed People of Color Killed by Police, 1999-2014. Retrieved July 11, 2016, from http://gawker.com/unarmed-police-of-color-killed-by-police-1999-2014-1666672349.

Learned Helplessness: Cherry, K. (n.d.). (What It Is and Why It Happens). Retrieved May 7, 2015, from http://psychology.about.com/od/lindex/f/earned-helplessness.htm

The Holy Bible

Somashekhar, Lowery, Alexander, Kindy, Tate J. S. (n.d.),.The 24 unarmed black men who have died in 2015; Ferguson: Police still killing unarmed black men one year later. (2015, August 8). Retrieved November 26, 2016, from *The Washington Post* from: http://www.washingtonpost.com/sf/national/2015/08/08/black-and-unarmedA162

Unarmed black people were killed by police 5x the rate of white people in 2015. (n.d.). Retrieved July 11, 2016, from http://mappingpoliceviolence.org/unarmed/

2016 shooting of Dallas police officers. (n.d.). In Wikipedia, the free encyclopedia. Retrieved October 04, 2016, from https://en.wikipedia.org/wiki/2016_shooting_of_Dallas_police_officers.

www.ingramcontent.com/pod-product-compliance
Lightning Source LLC
Chambersburg PA
CBHW060245290526
45789CB00001B/203